Melanchthon

MELANCHTHON

by ROBERT STUPPERICH

Translated by Robert H. Fischer

THE WESTMINSTER PRESS
Philadelphia

Melanchthon (German edition), by Robert
Stupperich, copyright © 1960 by Walter de
Gruyter & Co., Berlin

LIBRARY OF CONGRESS CATALOG CARD NO. 65–20620

Published by The Westminster Press®
Philadelphia, Pennsylvania

PRINTED IN THE UNITED STATES OF AMERICA

Contents

Translator's Preface

Philip Melanchthon has been an enigma from his own day to ours.

This layman composed the chief confession of Lutheranism and its chief theological textbook. He, not the outlawed Luther, was its chief negotiator in innumerable conferences between statesmen and theologians. He was the chief architect of Germany's school system. He was the only humanist with whom Luther in the long run remained on intimate terms.

He declined flattering offers from universities, kings, and Roman Catholic dignitaries to leave Wittenberg, yet he lived somewhat uncomfortably under the shadow of Luther. Especially after Luther's death, Melanchthon drew almost constant fire from theologians who accused him of selling out the Lutheran Reformation. Almost no one accepted his theological views completely. But just as surely, no one in Protestant Germany could get along without his versatile contributions to church, theology, education, natural science and the humanities, and even public affairs. He never received a doctor's degree, yet even in his lifetime he was acclaimed as " the preceptor of Germany."

Since his own day Melanchthon's reputation for the most part has remained under a cloud, or else has simply languished in obscurity. As for the picture of Melanchthon in the English-speaking world, it is difficult to say which writers have blurred it most — those who have ignored him, or his detractors, or his extravagant defenders.

In the following book, Robert Stupperich, probably the world's greatest living authority on Melanchthon, offers us a sympathetic, lively, judicious portrayal of the enigmatic man and his work. Through this readable, nontechnical account, readers will discover, Philip Melanchthon takes on a new historical importance, and the German Reformation a new focus and depth.

To Herbert Vogt, doctoral candidate and Assistant in the Bucer Institute at the University of Münster in Westphalia, I register my thanks for a number of corrections and suggestions that have improved my translation. I also gratefully acknowledge my debt to Dr. Peter Fraenkel, of the University of Geneva, in the preparation of the bibliography. Not only have I had access to his exhaustive international survey of Melanchthon literature (*Bibliothèque d'Humanisme et Renaissance,* 1960–1964) ; I have also profited from his personal advice.

Finally, my thanks to the author, Dr. Stupperich, who put his kindness and his learning at my disposal in answering several inquiries.

ROBERT H. FISCHER

Introduction

Cultural and Religious Life Before the Reformation

The years during which the young Melanchthon's basic views took shape were filled with those currents of Western cultural life which mark the end of the Middle Ages. These streams, which ran side by side and frequently mingled with one another, were the aftereffects of the great Scholastic systems, of the various mystical and ascetic tendencies, and of the German humanism with which they were in contact.

Long past was the age when men approached the church's doctrine with boldness and verve, and tried to establish its foundations before the forum of reason. No longer did men seek proofs of their truth and correctness. It was clear that faith and knowledge did not lie on the same plane. The achievements of medieval dialectics had long since advanced beyond this initial stage. Scholasticism had also promoted doubt and had produced other solutions than those which the church's doctrine demanded. True, the followers of Thomas Aquinas attempted to maintain his world-embracing system, but for the most part they contented themselves with a narrower theme. Their attempted unification of ecclesiastical doctrine and Aristotelian philosophy could not withstand the critique of a Duns Scotus. The acute Englishman had shaken men's

confidence in ecclesiastical science and its results. The
church could not prevent Scotists from appearing side by
side with Thomists at the universities, and it had to concede them equal rights. Although Thomas wished to derive everything from the intellect, Scotus on the contrary
regarded the divine will as the source from which all
things proceed. He no longer acknowledged governing
laws controlling the world. Even God's will is known only
where he wishes it to be known. The harmony of thought
and being is dissolved. Advancing along the same lines as
Scotus, his fellow countryman and fellow Franciscan, William of Ockham had shaken realism still more, and had
made it clear to his contemporaries that the doctrine of
the church cannot be proved on the basis of reason, but
can only be believed.

Scholasticism had dominated not only theology but all
intellectual life. Its methods, its art of dialectics, prevailed
in all realms in the universities and schools. Submission to
the church's doctrine was demanded of each field of knowledge. Scientific endeavor was not allowed to oppose it, but
had to seek conformity with it. If Scholasticism, on the one
hand, gave the church a consciousness of decisive power,
on the other hand, it also was destined to undermine this
foundation. No one dared to renounce the church's doctrine, even if many a person felt it as a fetter upon his
mind. Thus we see the Scholasticism of the waning Middle Ages accommodating itself to human abilities, and on
its own initiative restricting its earlier positions.

An attempt was made in Cologne and Heidelberg at the
turn of the century to revive the great traditions and to
prove Thomism the dominant school. "The Old Way"
(via antiqua), however, could not prevail in the face of
nominalism with its more modern critique of knowledge.

Cologne theologians from the Dominican Order, of whom Konrad Köllin is representative, tried to promote exclusively the teaching of their order's theologian, and other universities, such as the recently founded one at Frankfurt an der Oder, through the person of Konrad Wimpina, joined in these efforts. Most of the German schools, however, allowed both parties to exist side by side, in spite of this restoration movement. The newly revived Thomism was unable to bring forth new life. Only the antithetical views were occasionally sharpened. Hence, at several universities the adherents of each party were lodged in a special house (*bursa*) in order to stop the battle of opinions among the students. Nevertheless, at the end of the Middle Ages the rivalry of philosophical views was a feature of the German university, as it was customarily depicted, especially by Wimpfeling and other humanists.

In Tübingen, where Melanchthon attended theological lectures, he was stimulated by Ockhamism. These influences, however, were limited chiefly to psychology. The leading representative of this party, Jacob Lemp, was unable to impart to his students anything for their life, and he was regarded by them with a little pity. His dogmatic deductions impressed a Melanchthon as trivialities. The one thing that Melanchthon remembered from the lecture room of Lemp, and later recounted to his students, was the fact that the professor attempted to explain on a blackboard the Roman doctrine of transubstantiation. This recollection Melanchthon narrated with ironical remarks. To the preceptor of Germany, Lemp was the embodiment of Scholastic science: old, stunted, dead in its dry formalism. It seemed no longer equal to the life of the new age, so that men turned away from it, and instead emulated those who could offer worthy goals for life.

Melanchthon's parents had reared him in strict conformity to the church. The ideas of Geiler of Kaisers-
berg, the celebrated preacher of the Strassburg Cathedral,
had influenced his family. Geiler's sermons were read, and
they strongly affected the behavior of the members of the
family. In spite of his Scholastic schooling, Geiler knew
the world, and he had a taste for that piety which was
touched by the *Devotio Moderna* (Modern Devotion).
His sermons stirred both head and heart. Contemporaries
who sought the genuine and the true were receptive to
them. This pious attitude coupled itself with a natural
outlook and searched for a secure way through life. Geiler
had also espoused the cause of ecclesiastical reforms, and
like his friend the city clerk, Sebastian Brant, had sharply
criticized conditions in the church. We see how deeply
Melanchthon was attached to him during his early years
from the fact that in 1510, on the death of the famous
preacher, he composed a Latin poem, which is characteristic not only of the youthful student but also of the intellectual milieu in which he was growing up.

At the university, Melanchthon did not become acquainted with ecclesiastical learning at its best. This had
long since passed its prime, and only here and there did it
show a modest late bloom. Scarcely any significant expo-
nents of the church's doctrine were still to be found. True,
in Heidelberg the young Melanchthon had the opportunity of making the acquaintance of an amiable representative of Scholasticism in the person of his housefather, Pallas Spangel, and in Tübingen he walked in the footsteps of
" the last Scholastic," Gabriel Biel. The latter's theology
had a mild, conciliatory tone, but it did not succeed in
pointing out new ways and goals. Nothing about the current forms was upset; his intent was simply to gain from
them an intrinsic meaning and to give them a deeper inter-

pretation. Biel contented himself with preserving the tradition, cultivating the pious spirit, and striving after the original meaning of ideas.

With the mystical tendencies that in many places attempted to deepen theology and church life, Melanchthon obviously had no connections. Although Gabriel Biel in his old age had joined the Brethren of the Common Life and tried to introduce their way of life in Württemberg, similar efforts were not known in the Palatinate. Nor does it seem likely that young Master Philip was led along this path in Tübingen. Moreover, his older friend, Ambrose Blaurer, at this time joined not the Brethren but the Benedictines in Alpirsbach. The Modern Devotion with its Lower Rhenish character was not particularly popular in Upper Germany. The once significant mystical circles of the highlands had no influence any longer. The Friends of God plodded along in quiet inwardness, without further pondering the great thoughts of their founders. For the most part they were satisfied with rigorous admonitions in the manner of the " imitation of Christ," which afforded them support and comfort. This mood indeed brought fulfillment to some individuals, but no longer set great movements afoot. Important figures no longer arose in their midst. Only in attenuated fashion did the mystical mood persist in the broad strata of the populace, in Beguine houses, brotherhoods, and monasteries. Here, men continued to strive for an emotional, warm sincerity. But while Luther was later moved deeply by the sermons of Tauler and by the writing of the Frankfurt author, which he named " A German Theology," we hear of nothing similar from Melanchthon. On the way which he traveled, he did not come into contact with this world of spiritualization and inwardness.

Instead, his great-uncle, the famous humanist John

Reuchlin, had directed him toward other influences. Reuchlin apparently was familiar with the intimate questions in the mind of his grand-nephew. He referred him to Wessel Gansfort, whom he himself had once known in Paris and Basel. The latter maintained a critical attitude toward the church. He was prepared to regard the layman as highly as the priest and to concede authority to the word of Scripture alone. This critic, who closed his restless itinerant life with the Brethren in Deventer, had once affected Reuchlin strongly. Reuchlin also knew Nicholas of Cusa from his writings, and he had been with Gabriel Biel in Italy. The free attitude of Wessel Gansfort, and of his friend Rudolf Agricola, had imparted itself to Reuchlin. Their type of piety was thoroughly congenial to him. In Upper Germany others besides himself had adopted this outlook. Reuchlin now directed his model pupil Melanchthon to this piety. Though he allowed the lad to read only Wessel's writings, the older religious humanism nevertheless bore its fruit here.

During the very years when Melanchthon entered the world of scholarship, Reuchlin's controversy with the Cologne theologians ran its course. Although the converted Jew, John Pfefferkorn, demanded that the rabbis hand over the Hebrew sacred writings, especially the Talmud, Reuchlin had voiced his opposition in a memorandum. The controversy dragged out over many years, since both parties found supporters. There followed a legal action in Mainz and Speyer before the ecclesiastical court, and the publication of acts and opinions. The high point of this controversy was reached with Reuchlin's *Letters of Obscure Men*, published in 1515, in which the Cologne adversaries of Reuchlin were brought into ridicule in a caricature of the monks' Latin. The entire educated world of

that day burst into laughter over Cologne's obscurantism.
Reuchlin was the man of the hour. Understandably, Melanchthon stood at his side.

He owed it chiefly to Reuchlin that the world of humanism was opened to him. To be sure, he did not hold to
the ways of Reuchlin. Erasmus meant more to him.
Throughout his life the young humanist confessed himself
grateful to Erasmus. He felt a sense of liberation to be led
by Erasmus to an outlook which he could enjoy. Erasmian
humanism was built upon the foundation of the Sermon
on the Mount. In his *Manual of a Christian Soldier* (1501),
the prince of the humanists had set down and confirmed
his position. No longer confined by the Scholastic pattern,
he was able to unfold his ideas freely. The older German
humanists, of course, had also made a contribution in
opening up new paths, but Erasmus was the first to throw
open the door for all. Through him the new realms of
knowledge were made accessible. With him men returned
not only to the old, but also to the simple and natural. In
connection with scholarship, education came strongly to
the fore. Erasmus had succeeded in winning the younger
generation for a new ideal of scholarship. It devoured his
writings and followed his guidance not only to imitate the
ancients in beautiful style but also to gain new contents.
Now the German humanist could compete with the Italian. Now he had something of his own to offer, after Alex-
ander Hegius, Rudolf Agricola, and finally Reuchlin had
pioneered in this direction. In part through Erasmus' influence, the German humanist was shaped to a considerable degree by a religious outlook, though this characteristic was noticeable at the same time also in Italy and
England.

It must not be overlooked that German humanism in its

initial stage had close contact with the earnest way of life of the Brethren of the Common Life. Under the influence of this spirit several German universities were founded and regulated; aggressive men succeeded in putting through many of its demands. For decades, it is true, the " poets " had to fight with the " barbarians and sophists," before they could claim the final victory. The majority of them devoted themselves chiefly to education, and emphasized knowledge of the Bible and a moral life. Agricola had already succeeded in making the thought relevant: " Only the Holy Scriptures can lead us on a safe, reliable, proper way. They drive away every cloud, and they allow no one who follows their guidance to be deceived or destroyed."

Erasmus, however, was the first to gain widespread authority through his writing. He was often asked for advice, and he was able to exert influence on the political and ecclesiastical situation. Not only directly, but also through his numerous pupils and followers, he wielded power throughout all Europe. This influence stood in sharp contrast to his outward appearance. A short, timid man, always worried about his health, he nevertheless contrived to become a dominant power everywhere. He was frankly acknowledged as the spokesman of his age; he sensed the secret thoughts of his contemporaries; he furthered their desires and clothed their endeavors in proper form. If he was a man of piety, on the one hand, he left, on the other, the widest possible room for reason. He called his contemporaries back to clarity from everything extravagant and exaggerated. His brilliant style was a means to put across important ideas for the advancement of education and of life. Nothing escaped his sharp observation. Like other humanists, he often pointed out the abuses in the church. He ridiculed the work saints as " the new race of Judah," and strove to set up over against them his new ideal for man. Pure Christianity, the " philosophy of Christ," was based on the Sermon on the Mount. The ballast of tradition should be dropped in order that the original teaching of Christ and the apostles might shine forth. Erasmus pointed again and again to the Scriptures, for whose scientific study he created the foundation and whose interpretation he defined in his *Paraphrases.* True, in this effort he often failed to advance beyond pallid generalities, so that many regarded him as a mere stylist who had no conviction of his own. On most men, however, he knew how to impress the thought that the supreme happiness of all human beings is the cultivation of the mind, and the moral behavior that follows from it. Erasmus was the cultural aristocrat who felt a call to arouse the few and to lead them to truth. Melanchthon considered himself fortunate during his Tübingen period to receive personal recognition from Erasmus. Like all his companions of the same age, he was at first an Erasmian. In his attitude toward the church, of course, the traditional training from his home also played a role, but increasingly the religious outlook represented by Erasmus became his own. Like the majority of his generation, he regarded even Luther as in line with Erasmus. We do not know how he received Luther's Ninety-five Theses or whether he read Luther's tracts with the same excitement as Martin Bucer and John Brentz did. Nor do we hear why he did not rush to the Heidelberg Disputation. Apparently the distance between Luther and him was still great, and could be overcome only gradually.

I

The Development of the Humanist

1. HOMELAND, FAMILY, AND SCHOOL

In 1524, after six years as professor in Wittenberg, the young Melanchthon received from the elector his first leave of absence. On this occasion he visited his birthplace. Melanchthon's closest friend and first biographer, Joachim Camerarius, who accompanied him on the journey to Bretten, wrote a detailed description of the little town which at that time belonged to the Electoral Palatinate. He emphasized the beautiful site and the magnificent landscape, and he especially praised the astonishingly good buildings and fortifications. At the beginning of the sixteenth century, Bretten numbered not more than three hundred resident families, i.e., approximately two thousand inhabitants, and thus it took its place among the more important towns of the territory. It was not particularly rich. The citizens for the most part made their living by farming. Besides this, there was a reputable industry, chiefly weaving and tanning, and correspondingly a considerable trade, since the town was favorably located for commerce. Camerarius, who came from Bamberg, praised the way of life of the Bretten citizens, and called special attention to their morality and their lively cultural interest.

Melanchthon himself loved his homeland from the bottom of his heart. To the end of his life he felt most deeply attached to it. In a letter of August 20, 1545, he wrote: " The fruit of our life we owe first of all to those from whom we received it, our parents and our fatherland. By fatherland must be understood not only the soil which received us at our birth or the cottage in which amid our mother's great pain we came crying into the world. Rather, we have in mind at the same time the sacred places, laws, good institutions, and schools. For to these we owe our education, doctrine, understanding of moral behavior, and knowledge of God. These good things are worth more than life itself, and they must be preserved not only for our sakes but also for the sakes of our posterity. Thus it is easy to see that the well-ordered fatherland must be defended and must be protected and cherished like a mother, with all devotion."

To his fatherland, Melanchthon felt deeply indebted. When requests and inquiries from his homeland reached him, he always fulfilled them immediately, whether during the days of the Peasants' War, when the local peasants and the lord together named him arbitrator and he wrote a decision, or later in the midst of theological battles that he strove to clarify and bring to an end. " With a sigh," he wrote even in the last year of his life, " I often think of the hills and the fortresses which rise on the heights by the banks of the Neckar." His longing for his homeland became not weaker with age but constantly greater.

The same may be said of his feeling for his family. Melanchthon's father, George Schwartzert, was the elector's armorer. For a period he had been in the service of Emperor Maximilian, but then he had returned to his homeland. The emperor had conferred on him a coat of arms, which was used in his family, while the preceptor himself later selected his own coat of arms suitable for a theologian, inspired by John 3:14. Since George Schwartzert was often away with his lord, he could not think of establishing his own household very early. The elector himself had to intervene as matchmaker for his thirty-five-year-old armorer, negotiating his marriage with Barbara, the sixteen-year-old daughter of the Bretten mayor, John Reuter. The wedding took place in 1492 or 1493 in Speyer. Since the armorer still had to be away from home frequently, it was understandable that his wife remained at her large parental home in Bretten. There on February 16, 1497, her oldest son came into the world. In honor of the elector he received the name Philip. After him came a brother George and three sisters.

Following the custom of the time, his father had a horoscope cast for his eldest son by his friend the mathematician and astrologer, John Vierdung, of Hassfurt. Melanchthon, who attached great importance to the constellations of the stars, took his nativity seriously as long as he lived. " I fear the fates," he said, " even though I am no Stoic." Since Vierdung had thought that a course toward the north would someday bring him into danger and he would suffer shipwreck in the Baltic Sea, he always avoided a trip to Denmark. There is no need to interpret this inclination as a special superstition. It was a phenomenon of the times. At every princely court there was an astrologer, and even the most cultured men shared the views that antiquity had handed down to them. Melanchthon, as we see, had already absorbed this belief in his parental home, which was open to cultural influences. His grandfather, John Reuter, brother-in-law of the famous humanist Reuchlin, as a respected and widely traveled merchant had an appreciation of culture and the intellectual life, and he took part in the cultural activities of his time as much as he could. Moreover, his father, the " smith of Heidelberg," as he was called in Bretten, was no average artisan. Gunsmiths had considerable prestige, and had access to the courts of princes and to the higher nobility.

When he was only eleven years old, Melanchthon lost his father. After long illness the father, only forty-nine years of age, died on October 27, 1508. In loyal piety his famous son even in advanced years always remembered the day of his father's death. Contemporaries held that the incurable illness of which George Schwartzert died was the result of having drunk from a poisoned well in Mannheim during the Bavarian-Palatine War of Succession in 1504. Melanchthon remembered his father as a reserved, taciturn, and loyal man. So Philip described him to Camerarius. Severe suffering had left its mark on George Schwartzert and had refined him. He held strictly to the customs of the church. Even in the night he arose to pray. A few days before his death he gave his eldest son admonitions for his life; these hours Melanchthon always remembered with deep emotion. His father's pious and peaceful manner made a strong impression upon him. Never had his father contended with any man, nor had he ever gone before a court of law. His guardians decided that Melanchthon, mature beyond his years, should be spared from melancholy impressions attendant upon the death of his father; he was therefore sent to relatives in Speyer.

Melanchthon also frequently remembered his mother. Camerarius, who became acquainted with her in Bretten, called her a pious and intelligent woman. Left with five children, she did not have an easy time, especially since her father had died just ten days before her husband.

Though she lived in comfortable circumstances, many cares now fell upon her. Frequently Melanchthon mentions verses that he learned as a child from his mother. He must have been deeply attached to her, although he did not show his feelings. A correspondence with his mother, who died in 1529, has not survived. With his brother, Melanchthon maintained correspondence, and he apparently wrote to George twice a year, but of this material also only a small part remains extant. On the occasion when he visited his home in 1524, wrote Camerarius, the parting of mother and son was difficult. From the imperial diet at Speyer another visit in Bretten was possible; there Melanchthon saw his mother once more before her death. On this occasion, it seems, they discussed the question of church affiliation. Frau Barbara's piety was of a late medieval type, in which prayer and almsgiving played the greatest role. Her son advised her to keep on living in the same manner as before.

Of his childhood and parental home the future " preceptor of Germany " spoke seldom. He did not long enjoy the good fortune of living in a closely knit family circle. The long illness of his father lay like a shadow over his home life. It was apparently an orderly and well-to-do house in which he grew up. He never became acquainted with outward cares there. The period of sunny childhood, however, was only a faint recollection. The afflicted father could not devote himself to the education of his children; the grandfather had to take over this task. In the latter's house the young Melanchthon first came into contact with the culture and scholarship of his times. This was the world which appealed to him, and to it he devoted himself for the rest of his life.

Camerarius reports — and who could know better than

he? — that Melanchthon had a grave character. The account sounds improbable, and yet it cannot be doubted in view of Camerarius' intimate knowledge of Melanchthon. Melanchthon, he tells us, was all too inclined to sudden anger. However, he always composed himself and never acted in passion. This must have been a hard school for him, for in his later years we see him only as the mild — too mild — mediator, but never as the vehement and angry man.

Since Melanchthon in his letters occasionally expresses himself diplomatically, it is difficult to weigh his utterances one against another. At times contradictions thus emerge that cannot be reconciled. On the basis of such expressions, Ellinger went so far as to declare Melanchthon deceitful and to impute to him other defects of character. This judgment seems hardly convincing. Without question, Melanchthon is a complicated man who does not wear his heart on his sleeve; with all his caution and capacity for accommodation, his integrity cannot be questioned. There are many faults which one cannot overlook, but his honorable intention cannot be placed in doubt. He may have been quick-tempered, headstrong, indeed even harsh, but these characteristics appeared only when he saw the goal of his efforts endangered.

The reports of Melanchthon's schooling are not free from contradiction. The tradition, preserved by his colleagues in a " Brief Account " of 1560, relates that he attended the elementary school in Bretten, but then upon the outbreak of an epidemic of the French disease, carried by mercenary soldiers, received private instruction at home. This account rests on a legend. Apparently from the beginning he was educated, together with his younger brother, George, and other children, in a private school by John Unger, a teacher recommended by Reuchlin. Here he learned not only reading and writing, but also the Latin language. Unger must have been a strict and skillful educator; he imparted Latin grammar to his pupils by means of the poems of the neo-Latin poet Baptista Mantuanus. He did not spare the rod in his instruction. Nevertheless, Melanchthon always retained a grateful memory of this teacher, whom he later met again in Pforzheim. In Unger, despite his strictness, he sensed the genuinely fatherly love of the educator, and he knew how much he owed to his teacher. Unger demanded much and exempted him from nothing. That is why Melanchthon learned so much from him. As he himself said later, this man made him a philologist. None of his teachers were recalled in such warm words as Unger was. To a doorpost of his room he affixed the name Ungarus in order to bring repeatedly to remembrance this old teacher and friend of his family.

When Melanchthon's grandmother, Elisabeth Reuter, after the death of her husband removed from Bretten to her native town of Pforzheim, which next to Schlettstadt boasted the best Latin school, the two Schwartzert brothers were sent there for further education, probably upon the advice of Reuchlin. Since Philip Schwartzert had been excellently prepared in Bretten, he needed to remain in Pforzheim only one year. His teacher here was George Simler, a pupil of Reuchlin's, whom he soon thereafter met again in Tübingen as a professor. Simler also succeeded in imparting to his best pupils the elements of Greek, so that Melanchthon was eminently prepared in every respect for university studies. The " Brief Account " relates that Reuchlin often examined his grand-nephew, assigned him definite exercises, and was extraordinarily pleased with his progress. In Pforzheim, it is said, Reuchlin

also hellenized the name Schwartzert, according to humanistic custom, and gave the hopeful young neophyte in the
humanistic world the name Melanchthon. In other ways,
too, Reuchlin sought to promote him, sending him books
and thus stimulating him to further study. Melanchthon
kept in touch with many of his school companions for
years. It is astonishing how many well-known men came
from the Pforzheim Latin School: Simon Grynaeus, later
professor in Heidelberg, Nicholas Gerbel, Luther's intimate friend in Strassburg, and many others.

2. Course of Studies in Heidelberg and Tübingen

On October 14, 1509, Melanchthon was matriculated at
Heidelberg. The twelve-year-old lad was not regarded as a
prodigy, but studied as an equal among equals, especially
since there were many other young students besides himself. As at the Latin school, here also he must have practiced further the art of versification, for in 1510 upon the
death of the celebrated Alsatian preacher, Geiler of Kai-
sersberg, there appeared an *Epicedion* which he had
composed. In Heidelberg, Melanchthon lived in the house
of the theologian Pallas Spangel. It is hardly likely that
during these years he received any theological stimulation.
In later years he never says anything of this sort, but he
does mention the great humanists who had worked in Heidelberg before his time, in particular Rudolf Agricola. To
be sure, he found no trace of Agricola's spirit there any
longer, except that he heard of him from Pallas Spangel,
who had befriended him. Life in Heidelberg proceeded
quietly. Only one event during this period affected him
deeply. He relates that in the year 1511 he witnessed the

splendid wedding of Duke George of Pomerania and the Palatine Princess Amalie, which was celebrated with great tournaments of knights and festivities. On that occasion, as a page, he served as cupbearer to the Pomeranian knights who were quartered with Professor Spangel.

In the prescribed time of two years Melanchthon had earned the degree of bachelor of liberal arts. However, when he applied to win the master's degree at the age of fourteen, he was rejected because of his age and youthful appearance. Then the young student decided to transfer to another university.

Many reasons may have combined to draw Melanchthon to Tübingen in 1512: the death of Pallas Spangel, his own illness, the more favorable possibilities for his study. Here he found his old teachers Hildebrandt and Simler. Here Henry Bebel, a ranking humanist, the philosopher Stadian, and Stöffler, the astronomer, were still teaching. Tübingen offered him more than Heidelberg. A more lively academic life prevailed. Here there were stimulations for seriously inquisitive minds. In Tübingen, Melanchthon also gained two friends, both older than himself, who had the same interests as he had — John Husgen, of Weinsberg (Oecolampadius), and Ambrose Blaurer, of Constance, a monk in Alpirsbach.

This circle of friends read Erasmus. Melanchthon addressed a Latin poem to the admired idol of all the humanists, and the prince of humanists favored him with a fine, indeed warm, recognition. To be sure, it appears that what these men admired in Erasmus was the great philosopher and stylist. His " Christian philosophy " was not mentioned, nor were his reforming tendencies. However, Melanchthon did not lack an interest in metaphysics at this time. It was only a continuation of his previous development

that after earning his master's degree in January, 1514, he
also took up theological studies in addition to many others.
By this time Melanchthon's ambition for comprehensive
knowledge was already evident. Everything interested him;
he also pursued mathematical, juristic, and even medical
studies. But he cultivated these branches of learning more
by reading than by attending lectures. Reuchlin had advised him to read the writings of Gerson, and he had referred him especially to Wessel Gansfort, of Groningen,
whom he himself had learned to know and cherish during
his early years in Basel. At this time Melanchthon had also
received as a gift from Reuchlin a Latin Bible, which he
read eagerly, even in church during Mass.

As a young master, Melanchthon delivered lectures on
classical authors in his burse: Terence, Vergil, Cicero, and
Livy. He concentrated so thoroughly on Terence that in
1516 he could edit a new edition of his writings. After
Bebel's death he also received the professorship of eloquence that the humanist had held. He had already determined to follow his own path. It had become clear to him
that not only excellence in the form of speech was important, but also subject matter. As he pursued the objective
interpretation of the classicists, so he also desired not only
to use eloquence to adduce occasional examples from history, but to give this discipline ever more independence,
and he had already tried to sketch out and construct a theology of history. During these years Melanchthon worked
as corrector in the Anshelm Press. It fell to his lot to bring
into order the complex manuscript of Naucler, the first
rector of Tübingen, since interest was especially great in
this work, despite its considerable defects. When on a certain occasion in 1517 he had to deliver an address on the
seven liberal arts, he used the opportunity to underscore

the importance of history alongside of poetry.

Melanchthon also concentrated on philosophy. By comparing the Greek text of Aristotle with the Latin translation, he came to the conclusion that the Stagirite had been misunderstood in the Middle Ages. Thereupon with Stadian he conceived of the plan of preparing a new edition of Aristotle. Participants in the project were to be Reuchlin, Simler, Capito, and Oecolampadius. Here was already revealed a scientific spirit that was not satisfied to rest upon his past achievements, but used exact research, weighed all possibilities, and found new ways.

When Melanchthon in 1541 wrote the preface to the first edition of his collected works, he tried to describe his own outer and inner development. He related that he had begun to read poets and historians in Tübingen. Since he could learn nothing more there, he had begun to study independently. One gift, a present from Oecolampadius, proved especially useful: the newly published *Dialectics* of Rudolf Agricola. This book stimulated him profoundly in his academic labors. Agricola's method made it clear to him first how to establish basic concepts *(loci)*, and then how to deduce important viewpoints from them. It showed him how the context should be determined and in what order the topic should be treated.

Melanchthon was at peace with the theologians. However, the fact that he was counted as an adherent of Reuchlin, and that he had connections with the authors of *The Letters of Obscure Men,* altered the situation. The entire educated world saw itself threatened by the Cologne inquisitors. Melanchthon noticed how removed from reality the theologians of the day were, how much they lived in illusions. How false were the foundations of the old dialectics presented in the schools! In the main it led into a labyrinth and uttered nothing but ignorance.

Within a short time the situation of the young scholar had changed in Tübingen. Apparently he experienced snubbing and hostility. In May, 1518, in the foreword of his Greek grammar, he expressed himself bitterly over the academic situation as he encountered it. " The studies that should shape one's intellect and behavior are neglected, universal knowledge is nowhere apparent, what passes for philosophy is empty and fruitless deception which produces only contention. The true wisdom that came from heaven to guide the minds of men is banished."

Soon Melanchthon fell under suspicion. The intellectual atmosphere of Tübingen became too narrow for him, and his daily work in the burse became as oppressive as if he were in a workhouse. He thought that he could bear it no longer. Even Anselm's Press, in which he worked as corrector, brought him no stimulation but only burden. In retrospect in his later years all this appeared rosier again — the proximity to his homeland, the pleasant hours with humanistic friends, and the firstfruits of his intellectual creativity. At the time, however, he longed for another place of activity.

The aging Reuchlin, watching his richly gifted grandnephew from his home in Stuttgart, where he was active in the high court of justice, well recognized the yearning of his favorite pupil. " ' A prophet is without honor in his own country,' " he wrote him. When just at this time Reuchlin's personal friend, Elector Frederick the Wise, inquired whether he knew of a suitable Greek teacher for his University of Wittenberg, Reuchlin without hesitation recommended his protégé Philip and wrote to the elector, " I know of no one among the Germans who surpasses him except Master Erasmus." The elector felt obliged to call the recommended man. His answer was not long in coming: Melanchthon was given preference over Peter Mosellanus and called to Wittenberg.

Melanchthon did not find it easy to leave his homeland. Reuchlin himself felt the sadness of the separation. The famous humanist may have surmised what the distance would mean for the young master of Tübingen when he gave him the blessing of Abraham from Gen., ch. 12, as a godspeed.

After Melanchthon had taken leave of his family in Bretten he rode to Augsburg, where he presented himself to the Elector Frederick. Via Nuremberg and Leipzig, where the rising young star was splendidly feted by colleagues and friends, so that it was feared he might never reach Wittenberg, he resumed his journey and arrived on August 25, 1518, at the town on the Elbe.

II

The Way Into Theology

3. Beginnings in Wittenberg

On August 29, 1518 — it was a Sunday — the University of Wittenberg gathered for an academic act. The youthful Greek scholar from Tübingen, Master Philip Melanchthon, who had been called by the elector to the chair of Greek language, was to deliver his inaugural lecture. Among the expectant listeners was also Luther. The audience was not a little disillusioned when a small man with somewhat drooping shoulders mounted the rostrum. There was nothing imposing about the outward appearance of the new professor. He spoke with a stammer. Moreover, he had "a harsh and strident voice." Nevertheless, the address on the reform of studies which the young scholar delivered with such great inner involvement, and which set forth his entire program for Wittenberg, drew his audience along with him. Luther writes that they forgot his appearance and saw in him only the David who was destined to go forth against the Goliath of Scholasticism.

They were clear demands, which Melanchthon boldly and lucidly expressed. He entered upon his office with the intention of avoiding old, worn-out paths. The views that he brought with him from Tübingen were shaped by Aristotle. What did he want? To promote the genuine Aristotle, in order from this vantage point to take up the fight against Scholastic science and its method. Since men no longer drank from the sources, he argued, they had strayed far from the truth. Only so could it be understood that men had placed their precepts in the center of the stage instead of the gospel. Genuine erudition alone is able to distinguish the true from the false. Hence, he concluded, back to the sources, back to Holy Scriptures!

Melanchthon may have been naturally timid and cautious, but in his first appearance in Wittenberg he showed a courage that won all hearts to him. Where should the opposition to Scholasticism be more strongly and acutely felt than in Wittenberg? In this sign, Luther had already started on his way. And had not the humanists seen to it that this mood did not abate, especially among the youth? But there were also many battles to be fought, as the young Palatine certainly realized, for the advocates of the old way would not give up the field without a struggle.

Between Elector Frederick the Wise's court chaplain, George Spalatin, and Luther, both of whom had at first recommended another candidate, there still continued a correspondence over the question whether Melanchthon fulfilled the wishes of the university. Luther now abandoned his reservations over Philip's youthfulness and appearance. He knew that here he had the right man, whom God himself had sent him at just the right time. He declared himself unreservedly for " the little Greek," since he foresaw what Melanchthon would mean for Wittenberg. With his help, Luther hoped to succeed not only in bringing knowledge to a flourishing state but also in overcoming the crudeness of behavior that prevailed among the students on the Elbe, and in ushering in a new moral deportment.

The first wish was destined to receive fulfillment; with the
second task both struggled in vain, so that Luther almost
despaired for it.

Melanchthon found a new world in the flourishing town
on the Elbe. The difference from Tübingen was obvious.
The Wittenberg University, founded in 1502, had gathered a group of young, ambitious forces and learned
minds, and since Luther had opened a world-shaking battle, had attracted ever-growing crowds of students. The
outward conditions might not be elegant in every respect
— in comparison with the south German towns, Wittenberg with its simple houses looked like a village. Nevertheless, the frugal elector did equip his university after a
fashion, and took a personal interest in its development.
Here the waves of excitement surged higher than in Ingolstadt, Leipzig, or Tübingen, because a towering focus had
been found, to which both teachers and learners willingly
attached themselves. In Tübingen, Melanchthon had already made a name for himself as a dialectician. Now he
came to Wittenberg in the proud self-consciousness of a
humanist intent upon battle against everything barbarous.
He emphasized his responsibility as a philosopher concerned not with a beautiful object but with the truth of
which Plato speaks. From philosophy he hoped would
come every kind of improvement in life, and with Erasmus
he viewed religion as " the Christian philosophy."

Of course, his philosopher friends and Reuchlin himself
did not suspect that the circles into which Melanchthon
was about to be drawn in Wittenberg would estrange him
from their interests. The aged Reuchlin, no longer in a
condition to make a profound personal decision, had the
following year moved to Ingolstadt, where he lived in the
same house with John Eck, and he begged Melanchthon to

follow his example. When the call from Ingolstadt came, Melanchthon had already decided otherwise. A greater gift had become his than the library of Reuchlin, which he could have inherited. The advantages of Upper Germany he saw perfectly well. "I love my homeland," read his answer to Reuchlin, "but I must also heed whither Christ calls me, not whither my own pleasure may draw me." Nor did he hesitate to confess that now he could no longer be separated from Luther. "I will die rather than allow myself to be torn from Luther." Over this issue a break was inevitable, and Reuchlin expressed clearly enough his dissatisfaction over the behavior of his protégé: "Young people," he declared, "have no discretion." Apprehensive that he himself might be drawn into association with heretical Wittenberg, he told Melanchthon that he could no longer write to him.

It must have been no small surprise for Melanchthon to be received immediately as a friend in Wittenberg. It was not so much the many humanists as it was Luther himself who accepted him with greatest cordiality and openness. The confidence that the monk, thirteen years older than Melanchthon, reposed in him obviously laid him under obligation. In this strange environment it did him good to have met such a reception. Zealously embarking on his lectures in September, 1518, to which great crowds of students found their way, he was all the more thankful to have the opportunity of receiving instead of only giving. Here Melanchthon was to have time to concentrate and prepare for his coming greater tasks. At close quarters he could take part in the epoch-making events of church and world that would also prove determinative for his own career.

In September, Luther traveled to Augsburg for his hear-

ing before Cardinal Cajetan, to remain away almost five
weeks. He had departed from Wittenberg with grave
thoughts. Though he was received most kindly in Augsburg by humanist supporters such as Konrad Peutinger,
his letters reflect clearly the gravity of the situation. At this
time he directed his thoughts especially toward Melanchthon. He turned to him, since he saw in Melanchthon the
God-given continuator of his work. Scarcely were the ex-
citing events in Augsburg past, however, when further cri-
ses in church politics in which Melanchthon was to have a
direct part pressed into the foreground.

The dramatic proceedings that had taken place in Augsburg in October, 1518, did not blur Melanchthon's outlook. He felt that fundamental questions were at stake.
Contact with the new Wittenberg theology caused him to
delve into this area more thoroughly than before. The humanistic slogan, " Back to the sources," drove him to in-
vestigate the Bible still more intensively. According to one
thesis, Melanchthon during this time not only gained for
himself the clear awareness that the Scriptures furnished
the sole norm for Christian knowledge, but it was he who
influenced Luther to draw the conclusions which he did at
the Leipzig Debate: that there is no authority except Holy
Scripture; that neither popes nor councils have any importance in comparison with the Word of God — they have
validity only when they are in agreement with it. Scripture alone, Melanchthon declared, is pure and true, filled
with the heavenly Spirit, and therefore to be regarded as
the one and only touchstone.

If Melanchthon may have agreed with Luther in these
thoughts, there are also other ideas with which he may
have influenced Luther. The Wittenberg theology received considerable enrichment from Melanchthon and his

comprehensive historical knowledge. He advanced historical arguments in Luther's fight with the pope, and in general pointed out the importance of history for theology. Luther increasingly inquired into the subject. His historical studies before the Leipzig Debate were extensive. Under Melanchthon's influence he also provided the critique of papal law with a historical foundation.

4. THE LEIPZIG DEBATE AND ITS CONSEQUENCES

Indicative of the close relation in which Melanchthon stood to Luther was the fact that he rode with him in a wagon on the trip to the debate at Leipzig in June, 1519. Melanchthon himself had requested the elector's permission to accompany Luther. However little he liked theological disputation, in this case he took an intense interest in the controversy at hand. Melanchthon's alienation from Aristotle took place during the summer of 1519. Philosophical ethics he could characterize as the worst enemy of grace. He attended the debate in Leipzig only as a spectator. He had come along because he was convinced that here the decision must take place between the old and the new theology. It was clear to him on which side he belonged. Eck was annoyed that he made many whispered suggestions to the disputants.

When Melanchthon gave a report of the Leipzig Debate in a letter to his friend Oecolampadius, he revealed his personal position. He did not conceal his judgment, but gave clear expression to his views of the debaters and the interests for which they stood. To be sure, he acknowledged Eck's gifts, but the doctor's characteristic manner he found repulsive. What he beheld there was the kind of man called a sophist by the ancients. On the other hand, he made no secret of what attracted him in Luther, whom he now knew accurately from intimate acquaintance; in what measure he had already appropriated Luther's theology, he could not yet say.

Was Melanchthon forced into the arena against his will? Or had he not wanted, in awareness of his responsibility, to report to his friend Oecolampadius in Augsburg? That his letter was published and was destined to cause such a sensation, of course, he could not have suspected. Eck, suffering from offended ambition, issued a countertract; but he miscalculated when he thought he could dismiss Melanchthon as an insignificant grammarian. The answer of the humanist was sharp and cutting. Melanchthon laid clear emphasis on the principle that Holy Scripture can have only one meaning and dare not be obliterated by tradition.

With Luther's guidance, Melanchthon embarked upon new paths. After the Leipzig Debate his delight in the pursuit of theology had grown. Under Luther's leadership, new vistas opened for him. " I am completely absorbed in theological studies," he wrote to his fellow countryman Schwebel, " and they give me a marvelous pleasure." Now he was able to apply an order of priorities to his tasks. Thus he became the first philologist to devote himself wholeheartedly and in increasing measure to the exposition of Scripture. Besides his lecture on Homer, he was giving lectures on the letter to Titus. Though he never became free of a feeling of insecurity in theological work, he consciously intended from the beginning to cultivate theology, and so he wrote to Spalatin that he hoped he might accomplish something worthwhile in this realm.

In the summer of 1519 he began his exposition of the letter to the Romans, which he regarded throughout his

life, as Luther did, as the key to the New Testament. Here
his concern was not philological explanation, but as he
had learned from Agricola's dialectics and Erasmus'
method, the elucidation of basic concepts and the unfold-
ing of principal ideas.

How deeply Melanchthon had worked and lived his way
into the world of Pauline thought is shown not only by the
theses that he defended at his promotion to the degree of
" bachelor of the Bible " on August 9, 1519, and which understandably caused a sensation. No less is it revealed in
his address on the theology of the apostle Paul which he
delivered at the anniversary festival of the university on
January 25, 1520, in the presence of the electoral court
and of an imperial ambassador who was currently in Saxony. The decision had taken place. His judgment upon
Scholasticism became sharper. It cannot be asserted that
Melanchthon took up theology only with reluctance. This
notion arises from an exaggerated reading of his later
statements. On the contrary, his writings from these first
years in Wittenberg show with what inner conviction he
approached the exposition of Scripture and what depths of
the knowledge of God were opened up to him there. Precisely in view of these writings it must be emphasized that
Melanchthon drew conclusions from the Scripture with
greater consistency than Luther. Of course it is an exag-
geration to characterize him as the giver and Luther as the
receiver, up to 1519. Give and take stand in a mutual relation. Melanchthon was not so strongly bound to the old
ordinances of the church; hence, he was able to loose himself from them more quickly. Above all, he was concerned to set forth clearly the difference between what was
necessary for salvation and what was devised by men, and
consequently had to be abolished in the church. In the

latter category he included the sacrifice of the Mass, along
with the doctrine of transubstantiation. As Luther wrote
to Staupitz, he regarded Melanchthon's theses as daring
but true. The impression made by Melanchthon's disputation, in which he defended these theses, was generally a
strong one. " It was like a miracle to us all," added Luther.
" He will become the mightiest enemy of the devil and of
Scholastic theology."

On the side of the opponents also, men began to pay attention. The disputation theses came into the hands of
Eck, who immediately reported the bold author to his elector. " May your Electoral Grace for these reasons consider
well what error and heresy would arise if the matter is not
investigated." Thereupon Melanchthon once more set
forth and defended his rejection of the doctrine of transubstantiation in an open letter to John Hess, in Breslau.

5. THE DEFENDER OF LUTHER

Melanchthon stood unreservedly on the side of Luther,
who had opened to him the world of faith. He worked incessantly in order to assimilate everything that was offered to him. Naturally he appropriated not mere words
but new contents. Soon his expositions showed that he
spoke from his own experience. Ever more strongly did
Luther draw upon him as his collaborator. He even gave
him a share in his own literary work, since he was over-
burdened at this time. He could be confident that with
Master Philip instruction would continue uninterruptedly
at the university, and that no proofs from the printery
would lie idle. Melanchthon did everything: he edited Luther's explanations of the psalms, and also the brief Galatians commentary. In the prefaces which he added to

these works, Melanchthon said that he counted as fortunate the generation which now attended the university and could read such books, from which it could derive such great inward gain. Formerly it was the misfortune of Christendom that instead of Scriptural truth, sophistry was taught. So much had to be learned in Scholasticism that no time remained for the most important thing of all, the Word of Christ. Now, however, the great change had come. Now men had experienced it. Christianity was not an affair of science but of conscience, not of the intellect but of inner experience. "How does faith in God help you if you do not believe in his mercy?" One really came to know God only in his kindness. The Scriptures imparted that which was inaccessible to philosophy. Therefore Melanchthon admonished the students to immerse themselves in the Scriptures in order to win from them the correct understanding of the Christian faith.

For all the high esteem that Melanchthon still had for ancient philosophy and rhetoric, the difference in value between them and the Word of Christ had become clear to him. Human wisdom must not be an obstacle to understanding divine truth. To be sure, it was dangerous, as Luther's example shows, to take one's stand unreservedly before the truth of God, but the decision for it was required by the cause itself. Melanchthon saw it as Luther's task to excise all fantasies about the Scriptures and to let them exert in full their own effect. In his early writings he sought the way appropriate to him.

In the meantime Luther's case was running its course. Not in vain had Eck been busy in Rome. The bull of excommunication had appeared. In these dangerous times Melanchthon stood faithfully by Luther, without holding him back, since he saw that the affair had been started for

God's sake. To the burning of the excommunication bull
outside the Elster Gate on December 10, 1520, he had invited the students with the following notice: " Arise, pious
young students, come and attend this pious drama. Perhaps this is the time when the Antichrist must be revealed! "

At this time a Roman polemic came to the attention of
the Wittenbergers, addressed to the princes of the German
nation and designed to fill them with mistrust for Luther.
The author was Thomas Rhadinus, of Piacenza. Melanchthon immediately determined to write a reply to it. Behind the author, Melanchthon suspected, as did Luther
himself, Duke George's secretary, Jerome Emser, since the
tract had been reprinted in Leipzig. However dangerous
the situation threatened to become, Melanchthon had undertaken with firm resolution to defend the cause of the
gospel. Karl Sell has called this apology for Luther " Melanchthon's first Reformation writing." The tract was
completed within three months. It appeared under the
pseudonym " Didymus Faventinus." His investigations into
Peter Lombard proved useful in this situation. " We demand not sympathy or favor, but exact, strict testing," he
wrote, and continued: " Listen to nothing, you princes,
but the commandments of the Scriptures; think of nothing but your dignity and the welfare of your people! " He
succeeded in impressing upon the princes that Luther
never intended to destroy the peace, rupture Christian
unity, or start an uprising in the empire. As proof he narrated the origin and progress of the Reformation. His defense he ingeniously succeeded in shaping into an attack
against the doctrine of the Roman Church. Luther was re-
jecting not the old, but only those things which were devised in the medieval church as innovations. He stood for

the pure gospel, and applied it against the teachings of men. Melanchthon not only justified Luther's fight against indulgences; he penetrated to fundamental principles. Since he went back to Scripture alone, he turned his defense into an attack, similar to Luther's treatise *On the Babylonian Captivity of the Church*. "When I speak for Luther," he said in conclusion, "I speak for my holiest treasure, for the doctrine of Christ."

Not in vain had Melanchthon devoted himself to the Pauline views, which he now led into battle against Aristotle. What the latter taught on metaphysical and ethical questions, he rejected expressly, leaving only the natural scientific works valid. In Aristotle he found only dreams, whereas the truth was offered exclusively by Paul. Melanchthon had joined Luther in the fight against Aristotle. The task for which he had intended to work in Wittenberg was abandoned.

III

Struggle with the Powers of the Day

6. Results of His Theological Work

The dedications in the first writings which Melanchthon published in Wittenberg show that he had quickly established good relations with his colleagues. The *Rhetoric* and the *Dialectics* that he had probably begun to compose in Tübingen, and now sent to the press, soon caught the attention of the academic world and directed its eyes to the young scholar. Melanchthon published the *Rhetoric* first. He characterized it as the art of speaking correctly and well. In his judgment this ability presupposed certain kinds of knowledge. Rhetoric and dialectics differed only in form. In the preface to the *Rhetoric*, Melanchthon said: Everything depends on dialectics. It teaches the exact and artful investigation of a given subject, and its application brings light and order into all matters. On it depends not only the lucidity of a work; it first enables one to bring it under his control. The logic that ruled this field in the period of Scholasticism he renounced completely, just as Rudolf Agricola had done. Rhetoric and dialectics were contiguous for him, since both had a practical aim. The *Dialectics*, appearing in 1520, gained fame still more quickly. In the reorganization of Heidelberg University, Wimpfeling recommended its introduction as a textbook.

These two books were then published by the thousands of copies and eagerly studied by old and young.

In *Dialectics*, Melanchthon especially emphasized the finding of material (*inventio*). He summarized his view in the section on basic concepts (*de locis communibus*). A basic concept for him was nothing else than a common criterion by the help of which one could establish what deserved to be emphasized in a given subject. Since Erasmus in his *Method* spoke of *loci communes*, although in a different sense from Melanchthon, it is possible that he, along with Rudolf Agricola, had inspired Melanchthon to carry over this device into the realm of theology in order to emphasize and explain the most important material in this way.

Melanchthon had already applied this device in his first lecture on Romans. The copy that we possess of his *Theological Instruction* (*Theologica institutio*) shows us how he proceeded.

In the summer of 1519, when Melanchthon at Luther's suggestion expounded the letter to the Romans, he was at the same time busy with the printing of Luther's Commentary on Galatians. In the preface, which surely comes from him, he speaks of this book as the cord of Theseus which leads one through the labyrinth of the entire Scriptures. When he writes further of it that this book brings rescue to many who have suffered shipwreck on the ocean of Scholastic distinctions, it is his personal experiences that are expressed. Now Scripture has recovered its splendor through Luther and reveals its power for men's minds; the light of Christ illumines the Biblical books and points out the way to every man.

He who longs for salvation, says Melanchthon, finds the truth therein. For this reason Luther's writings, of all those

which hold fast to the Bible, also deserve to be read, for he
has succeeded most profoundly in bringing to expression
what the apostle Paul is talking about. Melanchthon mar-
vels at the enormous work of Luther, who did not spare his
energies but devoted them all to expounding the divine
Word. He emphasizes that he has read over Luther's com-
mentaries several times, and has changed what he found
needed changing. Particularly does he emphasize Luther's
exposition of the Pauline doctrine of justification. The Reformer has approached the Scriptures without prejudice,
he asserts, and has disclosed its riches. In these words lies
Melanchthon's personal testimony of how he has been led
by Luther into the profundities of Scripture, and how in
this way he has attained understanding and experience.
Why does one read the Bible, he asks, if not to comprehend the meaning of justification? Of what use is it to
know that God is merciful if one's own heart is not
touched by the realization " that he is merciful to *you* "?
To have this experience is " to know God truly."

That Melanchthon did not simply repeat Luther was
clear to his hearers and readers. Luther, too, was aware of
it. How highly he valued Melanchthon's theological explanations is shown by the fact that he would have liked to
send all the monks in his cloister to hear his lectures. He
was firmly convinced that Melanchthon in this respect also
could accomplish more than he himself could, indeed,
more than several men like himself.

This knowledge Melanchthon has gained from the letter
to the Romans: the most important questions with which
theology has to do are sin, law, and faith. In the treatment
of them it becomes clear what justification is and what it
means. What can men do, over against God's activity?
" Philosophy is in no position to change the minds of men

and to bring about an inward renewal." This fact had already been established by the apostle Paul: by his own powers man cannot become righteous. He resists the law, and this simply misleads him into works righteousness. Then God himself intervenes in his mercy and sends Christ to win for man his salvation. In faith in Christ, however, man becomes righteous, his conscience is quieted, his inner powers are renewed. Melanchthon finally makes clear the difference between the Christian and the heathen understandings of righteousness, and closes with a eulogy on faith.

Master Philip was already aware of the basic ideas of the doctrine of justification. Still lacking was its necessary connection with other doctrines. One can say, nevertheless, that his words echo his personal experience: " O enormous benefit, so to know Christ that he takes away your burden when you are oppressed by the law and your consciousness of guilt, and sets you on his shoulder, that he sustains you when you thirst for righteousness — happy are those who have attained so to know Christ! O unreason, O darkness, to seek comfort elsewhere for the sorrowful conscience, to expect righteousness and holiness elsewhere than from Christ! "

For a full-scale presentation, however, the draft of the *Theological Instruction* did not suffice. For this purpose Melanchthon sketched another plan. On this basis he began a detailed development of his project. He had no interest in writing a commentary on the letter to the Romans. He wished to express that which dare not be forgotten in reading the Holy Scriptures. As Luther later in the Smalcald Articles left aside the " articles concerning the divine majesty " and started immediately with the article on justification, so Melanchthon also says here that no discussion over God, the Trinity, and the Incarnation is possible. Christ, rather, came into the world in order to lead men to a knowledge of God and of their situation before God. " This is Christian knowledge, that one knows the demands of the law; if one knows from whom the power to satisfy the law and from whom the forgiveness of sins are to be implored, and how one's wavering spirit can be strengthened against the devil, the flesh, and the world, and one's shattered conscience comforted. . . . Therefore we propose to sketch a system of basic concepts that should bring Christ closer to you, strengthen your conscience, and establish your soul against Satan." Melanchthon leads through the exposition of details to a comprehensive presentation of evangelical knowledge.

Upon him, as also upon many of his contemporaries, Luther's chief writings of 1520 had exerted the strongest impression. Under the influence of this impression Melanchthon wrote his _Loci Communes_. Consciously he departs from traditional dogmatics, even though he refers to them. He starts with the portrayal of man: natural man has no power for good. Through the Fall he has lost his love for God, and he allows himself to be led by selfishness. From then on the root of his actions is sin. Even his love is poisoned by selfishness. He does not attain salvation through free will, but only according to God's predestination.

God gives man the law, in order that he may know himself and become aware of the perversity of his heart. He cannot fulfill the demands of the law, and must therefore despair. In this situation the gospel reaches him — the word of forgiveness and of new life. If a man believes the divine promise that Christ does everything for him, and does not doubt that Christ's righteousness is his righteousness and Christ's sacrifice is an expiation for him, then he is justified. " To know Christ is to know his benefits."

Melanchthon also inquires more closely into the nature of faith. Like Luther, he sees it in trust and in the readiness to serve God and one's neighbor. In this service, faith proves its genuineness. Here we have reverberations of Augustinian ideas, but they are more originally conceived and are reinterpreted.

The contrast of law and gospel also stems from Augustine. Melanchthon attempts to bring out this antithesis more sharply than Luther does. In this context he emphasizes the importance of the law, and asserts that the gospel cannot be preached without the law. The new man, who is filled with the Spirit of God, indeed needs the law no longer.

Only faith justifies, not the Sacraments; the latter are only signs of the promises and gifts of God, given for the comfort and strengthening of weak consciences. Melanchthon speaks in the *Loci* of only two Sacraments: Baptism and the Lord's Supper. Baptism leads one out of the consciousness of sin to the certainty of grace. A special sacrament of repentance Melanchthon deems unnecessary. The Lord's Supper he interprets as a sign of grace for the comforting of consciences. Melanchthon closes his book with several chapters on ethics, in which he makes it clear how faith and love have to prove themselves in the world.

This work, which Melanchthon had handed over to the printer in April, 1521, could not be steadily put through the press until completion. The printed sheets appeared at long intervals and were sent singly to his friends. Luther read them at the Wartburg. The delay was caused not only by outward events. Melanchthon was confronted with new questions by Luther's book against Latomus, and he had to settle them. In the letters exchanged between them at this time, Melanchthon's inner situation is clearly revealed. The reading of Luther's book caused him to make many alterations and insertions, through which the unity of his original conception was destroyed. In this connection, moreover, it dare not be overlooked that Luther admonished him from the Wartburg to bear his cross patiently. Even that famous principle — he must proclaim no imagined grace, but genuine grace, and must comprehend sin not as ideas but as reality — is not to be connected to the outward happenings in Wittenberg only but also to his inner development.

Melanchthon himself was not satisfied with his book, which appeared in December, 1521. At many points it was too elementary. Thus he also did not wish to be called Master. Even though this first attempt to expound the Christian faith upon an Evangelical foundation showed many weaknesses and defects, on the whole it was a magnificent book. The enthusiasm of friends and the repugnance of enemies is thus easy to understand. The doctrine of the Reformation had been impressively treated in a few chapters. Luther's admiring judgment that this little book deserved to be regarded as canonical overshot the mark. It must be said, however, that it not only brought about a conversation with the past, but also opened the way ahead. It followed a line of its own, and can by no means be regarded simply as a summary of Lutheran ideas. It also contained humanistic features; as a matter of fact, it is characteristic of Melanchthon that throughout his life he consciously or unconsciously took into account the heritage of German humanism and the influences of Erasmus. It was his manner of bringing Biblical ideas to expression, however, that made the greatest impression upon his contemporaries. His presentation is always clear and the Biblical foundation convincing. The book was read to an extraordinary extent. In four years eighteen editions appeared.

7. AGAINST FANATICS AND BAPTISTS

Before the hearing with Cajetan, Luther had envisaged Master Philip as his successor, and commended to him his work. So, now, from the Wartburg he could think of none of his Wittenburg friends who could so effectively take his place as Melanchthon. " Step forward as the servant of the Word; guard the walls of Jerusalem! " So ran Luther's charge to him. But it was exactly this guiding hand which Melanchthon lacked. In this respect Luther overestimated him. In his letters to Spalatin he suggested that Melanchthon should be installed as preacher in his place. According to his conception, Spalatin could see to it that the town council would call Master Philip as preacher. Such a call Melanchthon would not be able to turn down. Melanchthon, however, did not acquiesce in this proposal, whether he knew that he was not cut out for such work or whether his congenital impediment in speech deterred him. He was unwilling to exchange the lecture desk for the pulpit. In the university, moreover, this twenty-four-year-old professor was one of the most highly respected scholars. His acuteness and ability, his gifts of organization and clear formulation, were much esteemed.

The results of the Diet at Worms had not shaken Melanchthon's attitude toward Luther. He remained more firmly attached to him than ever; indeed, he was able to encourage others. Shortly before this he had completed his reply to the Sorbonne, which had finally published its

judgment on Luther and had tried to trace his theology
back to ancient heresies. It was characteristic of Melanchthon to give his answer promptly. " False theologians " he
called the members of this far-famed faculty, which delivered no verdict of its own but only tried to hide behind
the authority of the church fathers and councils. Melanchthon declared, on the contrary, that Luther not only had
the Holy Scriptures on his side, but also could claim the
support of the most important church fathers, such as Augustine, Hilary, and Chrysostom. If many of his utterances
could not be proved from the ancient fathers, that was
connected with the fact that the ancient church was not
yet so corrupted as the present church. The same thing, he
said, was true of the councils. Although Luther agreed
with the ancient church synods, he contradicted the later
ones which declared themselves contrary to the Scriptures.
On the whole, his doctrine agreed with the Christian
church, but opposed Aristotle and all the philosophy of
the schools. The condemnation of Luther which the Sorbonne had undertaken, Melanchthon declared worthless
because it could not prove its verdict, and especially since
it was ignorant of the Scriptures and Augustine.

Luther himself had predicted to Melanchthon from the
Wartburg that his enemies would now attack Melanchthon
also. This battle Melanchthon accepted. He wrote in im-
passioned tones, for what was at stake was not only his ex-
communicated friend, but the cause that was also his own.
Luther's deed had brought a certain relief to him as well.
This must now come to expression. What no one had dared
to say clearly for four hundred years, Luther had said. Melanchthon saw this event in a broad framework: God's
mercy had again shone forth, his gospel had been revealed
to his people, and the conscience of those whom he had
called had been strengthened. Melanchthon put it so in his

tract against the Sorbonne: If you ask how Luther has
served the church, then learn these main facts: he has
taught the true manner of repentance and has shown the
right use of the Sacraments, as the consciences of many men
can testify to me.

It is easy to understand that Luther in his loneliness felt
invigorated by this confession of his theology. For this reason he translated this personally written tract of Melanchthon into German at the Wartburg. Other common problems also had been touched by Melanchthon. While Luther
was writing the treatise *On Monastic Vows,* Melanchthon
also turned his attention to the same theme. Occasion was
furnished by the marriage of Provost Bernhardi, who had
been brought to trial because of it. Melanchthon's defense
caused a great sensation everywhere. Repercussions were
noticed in Luther's monastery. And as long as an eloquent
monk, Gabriel Zwilling, aroused excitement there and
poured oil on the fire by his preaching, Melanchthon could
do nothing to quiet it. Probably he did not even recognize
what kind of person Zwilling was, and he at first approved
of his views. Then, however, he decided to clarify the situation by a disputation on October 17, 1521. In his theses
he emphasizes the basic importance of the Word in the
Sacrament, and indicates after Luther's manner, that the
Sacrament appropriates the promised grace to the individual. It is a sign, but no work and no sacrifice. The traditional form of the Mass overlooks the decisive point and,
as he says further in his theses, inevitably produces spiritual blindness. Melanchthon essentially upholds the action of the Augustinian monks and takes his stance against
any appeasement, quoting Luke 9:62, " No one who puts
his hand to the plow and looks back is fit for the kingdom
of God."

On instruction from the elector an investigation was

made into the happenings in the Augustinian monastery
and Melanchthon was summoned to report. He used this
opportunity to underscore the necessity of replacing the
order of the Mass with the original form of the Christian
Lord's Supper. With all definiteness he called upon the
elector to permit this new order so that he might not be
rejected at the Last Day. Frederick the Wise, however, decided that precipitate action must be avoided. Such an in-
terference with the system of worship could not possibly
have taken place in Wittenberg alone. Meanwhile, the
fight against the Mass had spread, as professors and students took part in it. In early December, 1521, Luther
made a secret visit to Wittenberg. He stayed at Melanchthon's, and discussed events and measures with him. This
is clearly reflected in his tract, *An Earnest Exhortation for
All Christians*. It was Melanchthon who at this time induced him to take up the work of translating the Bible
into German at the Wartburg. In this situation, moreover,
Melanchthon had no intention of mitigating the battle
with Archbishop Albert of Mainz.

In September, Albert's chancellor, Wolfgang Capito, had
come to Wittenberg to attempt a reconciliation. The Erasmian official intended to work on Melanchthon especially.
He deplored Luther's vehemence and expressed the wish
that he would temper his speech. Melanchthon, however,
upheld Luther completely. " I know," he said, " that some
regard him as a bad man and others as a foolish one. But I
am convinced that he pursues his work not merely with
wisdom but also with the best possible conscience, particularly since he seems to have been destined to it by God."
Luther's principle of the sole authority of Scripture was
immovably fixed for him, and he opposed Capito over its
alleged obscurity. He also attacked the traditional Scholas-

tic view of man. If the free will is not repressed, he declared to him, grace is obscured. During those days Melanchthon acted so boldly for Luther that all caution appeared to him as cowardice. Later, recalling this conversation with Capito, he said: " One kind of man I dislike intensely — that is the men of wise and pious appearance who enjoy great success in word and writing and try to improve themselves and others, yet carefully sidestep everything offensive. If Paul had taught only that men should lead an upright life, the princes of this world and the false apostles would have received him with open arms. But when he condemned works righteousness and the shallow moral views of the great world, Pharisees and whole nations rose up against him. In just the same way Luther would be regarded as one of the wisest and holiest of men if he would write a lot of pious stuff but avoid assailing what is offensive about the pope and human commandments and the Mass." When Luther urgently called on Archbishop Albert to abolish the indulgence in Halle, Melanchthon also appended a letter to Capito. This letter is a renewed testimony of his support for Luther: " You cannot deny," he emphasizes, " that he teaches the gospel; if you repulse Luther, repulse this also! "

Karlstadt and Zwilling, meanwhile, decided that their time had come. With great fanfare they carried through the innovations that they considered necessary in the church. Melanchthon did not want to be influenced by them, but he also made no effort to stop them, in the conviction that everything now must be left up to God. On December 27, 1521, however, some weavers from Zwickau had appeared in Wittenberg and had come to Melanchthon. Their chief interest was the immediate guidance of the Holy Spirit. They believed that he who possessed the Spirit needed the

Biblical Word no longer, that he stood under direct divine
guidance. In the face of this fanaticism, Master Philip was
defenseless. He confirmed that they were filled with the
spirit, but he did not know which spirit this was. Therefore he did not dare to pass judgment and issue a verdict.
Immediately after this meeting he wrote to the elector and
requested Luther's return. One thing, at all events, he per-
ceived already, that the enthusiasm of the Zwickau men
rested on self-stimulation and self-deception. The behavior of the former university student Mark Stübner, who
lived at his house, helped him to arrive at this conclusion.
The fact that the Zwickau prophets abolished child Baptism and shifted the chief stress from faith to possession of
the Spirit made him regard their attitude as scarcely tena-
ble. Luther, upon receiving news of the fanatics' appearance and their criticism of child Baptism, from the first
took a more serious view. He also exhorted Melanchthon
to " test the spirits to see whether they are of God." God's
revelation, he said, takes place under terror. Knowledge of
heavenly truth comes to a person only through deep inner
struggle.

This counsel Melanchthon seems not to have followed.
While he held back, Karlstadt stepped into the foreground.
He approached the Zwickauers and showed himself open to
their tendencies. Their provocative speeches led to the
smashing of images in the town church. On receiving this
news the elector sent word to Melanchthon that he should
curb Karlstadt and Zwilling. But this admonition no
longer helped. Melanchthon himself had now reached the
conclusion that a single individual could no longer stem
the tide. With several changes, such as the removal of images, nothing was accomplished. All signs pointed toward
a storm. In this movement divine and human elements

threatened to become confused. Already Melanchthon feared " that the light which had risen in the world only a short time before would soon disappear again before our eyes." Through a messenger he informed Luther how tense the situation had become and how little he could do against it. On March 3, 1522, he had his answer: Luther had determined to return to Wittenberg.

The controversy with the fanatics was now brought to an end within a few days, and the path was once more free for the revision of the order of worship and for the regulation of practical church problems. It was clear that the Mass could no longer be practiced in the old manner. Luther accepted Melanchthon's suggestion to retain the old pattern except at those places relating to the sacrifice. In the liturgical work Melanchthon took no part. Before Luther sent to the press *The New Testament in German,* which he had prepared at the Wartburg, he once more worked it over quietly with Melanchthon on the basis of the Greek text. Thus, besides suggesting this work, Master Philip also had a considerable part in shaping it. Every detail was carefully tested, both for concepts and for contents, and in this manner the work was completed which made its way to the people as the *September Testament* of 1522.

The Wittenberg riots had greatly damaged the academic life of school and university. Now the work had to be resumed and led into orderly paths. Melanchthon extended still further the theological lectures that he had taken over as Luther's substitute. In the latter's absence he had first expounded the letters to the Colossians and Second Corinthians, then the Gospel of John. Moreover, he had to discharge the duties of his own professorship in the Arts faculty, so that his energies were strained to the utmost. In the outward controversies he had experienced what inner struggles were involved.

If Melanchthon even earlier could not come to an agreement with Karlstadt, he now regarded the latter's influence with the deepest mistrust. The fanatical trait persisted in Karlstadt and drove him in the spring of 1523 to open an attack against Luther. He also set himself against all kinds of learning, so that Melanchthon found himself actually forced to point out to the youthful students in his academic addresses the necessity of studies. Later also, when Karlstadt was up to his tricks again in Upper Germany, Melanchthon separated himself from him in the sharpest possible manner. For mystical fanaticisms of any kind, he had no taste. Further, he credited Karlstadt with no genuine integrity, but saw in him primarily impure motives.

Whether Melanchthon also came to know Thomas Müntzer in 1522 is not certain. Before Müntzer turned against Luther, he wrote to Melanchthon. There were tones which to the latter were not unfamiliar from the Zwickau prophets. Men should pay no attention to the outward letter, but listen to the inner Word which God speaks to the living soul. "Believe me," Müntzer concluded, "that God speaks much more readily than you are ready to hear." In his rejection of the fanatical spirit, Melanchthon was in agreement with Luther. In Wittenberg not only with the Zwickauers but also with Karlstadt and Müntzer, he had learned where this conceited spirit led. To make clear to the people the consequences of fanaticism, Melanchthon later wrote a popular *History of Thomas Müntzer*. Without going into the deeper roots of Müntzer's views, he only wished to show in this writing to what end Müntzer was led by his fanaticism. His own conviction remained firm: everything that bore the semblance of spiritualism he bluntly rejected. The judgment that he had formed of the Zwickauers and fanatics he later carried over into his views of the Baptists.

Later controversies strengthened him in the view that with the Baptists one had to deal with the same phenomenon as with the Zwickau prophets. Melanchthon saw no reason to revise this view, but held this conviction throughout his life. The numerous memoranda that he prepared concerning spiritualists and Baptists all proceed from this basis. Whether it was rationalistic or enthusiastic motifs that were more at stake, he did not care. He saw in them men who treated the Biblical revelation with contempt. In his eyes they were disseminating new teachings that would corrupt the planting of God. Not only the different exposition of Scripture but also the different conception of the Sacraments played a role in his attitude. Like Luther, Melanchthon emphasized that God demanded that a man look first to him, not to himself. To this end God equipped him with his gifts, as weapons against unbelief, despair, and death. Such a gift, to a special degree, was Baptism, whether for children or adults — no empty sign, but a sign of divine grace. The Baptists, on the other hand, in his opinion taught only uncertainties and presented basically a doctrine of works without Christ.

His impressions from the church visitation tours also led him to take up this task — the controversy with the Anabaptists — which was regarded as urgent in the congregations. Melanchthon wrote a comprehensive Latin memorandum on the question of Baptism, which was translated into German by Justus Jonas and widely circulated as a tract.

In his doctrine of Baptism, Melanchthon also speaks of the repentance that teaches us to see in Christ God's wrath

against sin. The cross of Christ shows the greatness of the
divine wrath. Therefore, he who lives without repentance
and the fear of God desecrates Baptism. For in Baptism on
the one hand we receive a judgment upon ourselves, but
at the same time it grants an insight into the promised
grace of God. Hence, when the conscience fights despair, it
needs to remember Baptism as the " testimony of promised grace." Thus Baptism is the way out of spiritual tribu-
lations to freedom, to life, and to glory. The spiritual fanatics, of course, repudiate this view — on the grounds of
reason they also reject child Baptism. Melanchthon com-
bats their views even on the basis of the Old Testament,
and strives more than ever to make the ancient church's
practice of child Baptism convincing from the New Testament. If Scripture does not expressly command that children are to be baptized, neither does it forbid child Baptism, so that the church's practice seems not without
foundation.

Melanchthon knows that many other objections are to be
raised against the Anabaptists, that in their fanaticism they
violate other ordinances of ecclesiastical and civil life. The
root of their error, he judges, is that they neglect the First
Commandment and allow themselves to be guided by self-
love.

IV

Labors for Church and School

8. Transition to New Tasks

The labors that burdened Melanchthon had greatly undermined his health. His friends were anxious for the Master, who knew only work without regard for his outward welfare and circumstances. Luther accordingly wrote to Spalatin as early as the summer of 1520 that the young professor needed a wife who would take care of him and a homelife in which he could be happy. The Wittenberg climate and the heavy diet, moreover, did not suit him. Melanchthon himself at first rejected the demands of his friends, since he feared that he would have to cut down his studies if he were to devote enough attention to a wife. His friends, however, did not give up. The wedding took place on November 25, 1520. Melanchthon married Katherine, the daughter of the Wittenberg burgomaster and tailor Hans Krapp. Through this marriage he became a brother-in-law of his two colleagues Augustine Scheurl and Sebald Münster. Katherine Krapp was the same age as her husband, an upright and faithful wife whom Melanchthon could not praise highly enough. To be sure, it was difficult for him at first to adapt himself to his new situation. Soon, however, he realized what grace God had imparted to marriage in giving each of the partners the opportunity to be concerned for the other. Katherine Melanchthon had only one fault: she did not know how to manage a household. There was never money in the house, because she was just as liberal as her husband. Sometimes, therefore, chaos would have prevailed in the home if Melanchthon had not had in John Koch the most efficient assistant (*famulus*) that he could imagine. This man not only helped him in scholarly labors but also assisted in the housekeeping. From year to year the family grew. Melanchthon was attached to his children with deep love. Visitors sometimes saw him with a book in his hand, sitting at the baby's cradle. For his pupils and guests also, however, he always had time.

Two qualities of Master Philip must be particularly emphasized: his capacity for concentration and his conscientiousness. His achievements are understandable from the fact that he was able to work quickly and without interruption. Students streamed to his lectures, which he never canceled without good reason. His hearers learned about his wedding through the following poetic notice:

> Today Philip happily takes a holiday from studies.
> He will not lecture to you on Paul's holy doctrines.

In 1520, Spalatin counted over five hundred students in his theological lectures alone, and in all his lectures together over fifteen hundred. No one else in Wittenberg had such academic success. Melanchthon had thrown himself unreservedly into his tasks, and had not spared his energies. Now Luther, too, thought it appropriate that he should take a rest in his homeland. The elector granted him a leave of five weeks. Accompanied by four friends, including Camerarius, Melanchthon made this journey by horse in the summer of 1524. Through Leipzig, Fulda, and

Frankfurt led the road to his native Bretten. Camerarius reports that when Melanchthon caught sight of the little town he dismounted from his horse, knelt, and cried out with deep emotion: " O my native land! How I thank thee, Lord, that I may set foot in it! " While his friends rode farther to Basel in order to visit Erasmus and Oecolampadius, Melanchthon remained at his mother's home. There were definite reasons, however, why he did not pay a visit to Erasmus. The controversy of Erasmus with Luther over freedom of the will had cast its shadows ahead, so that he preferred to avoid a cool reception in Basel.

Unexpectedly there came to him in Bretten an honor from the University of Heidelberg. As emissaries of the faculty of arts, Hermann von dem Busche and Simon Grynaeus delivered to their now-famous colleague a silver goblet. The faculty wished to make him forget that he had once been denied the master's degree. He received another visit also. From Stuttgart appeared Frederick Nausea, the secretary of Lorenzo, Cardinal Campeggio, who by order of the legate made offers to induce him to go over to the other side. Melanchthon's answer was clear, much as he emphasized his love of peace. He would continue to set forth the pure doctrine, and wished only that all who had the church's welfare at heart would unite to amend the intolerable conditions in the church. For the legate Melanchthon jotted down a brief note on Luther's doctrine. " The world errs if it says that Luther wanted to abolish church practices. Luther does not fight over outward things. His concern is the righteousness of God. Scripture alone, to which he appeals, can confirm the conscience against the gates of hell. Human traditions contribute nothing toward the righteousness of God. In the Mass there are so many abuses that they cannot be overlooked. If no changes are

made in it, then men who are far from being Luther's pupils will arouse people against the church."

When Melanchthon's traveling companions returned
from Basel, he made the journey back with them. In the
Odenwald not far from Frankfurt they met the young
landgrave, Philip of Hesse. Philip was reputedly an oppo-
nent of the new teaching. He amused himself by alarming
Master Philip. He took him captive. Then he asked him
to accompany him to his inn. A whole night they kept up
a conversation over questions of faith. In the morning the
prince released him with the condition that Melanchthon
should soon send him a written statement of the Evangelical faith.

This task Melanchthon took very seriously. Immediately
after his return he wrote for the landgrave an *Outline of
the Restored Evangelical Doctrine*. In it he refers to the
fact that many misunderstandings in regard to Luther's
doctrine are current among his contemporaries. The gospel alone furnishes the test for this teaching, whose focuses
are to be found in righteousness and in works. The Christian's righteousness consists in the fact that his terrified
conscience receives consolation through faith in Christ.
This consolation of the forgiveness of sins becomes his
through the gospel. Therefore the gospel must be preached
and not suppressed. It remains an open question whether
this *Outline* settled Landgrave Philip in his decision and
thus prepared the way for the Reformation in Hesse,
which was introduced soon thereafter. The landgrave's
personal relations with Melanchthon continued from then
on through four decades. Though Melanchthon declined
a call to the University of Marburg, founded in 1527, he
remained on many occasions the adviser of the landgrave.

The journey to his homeland had revived Melanchthon's connections with the Palatinate. When the peasants' uprising burst upon the land in the spring of 1525, the peasants themselves had proposed him as arbitrator between them and the lords. Elector Ludwig had promised them to have their Twelve Articles examined, and then had begged Melanchthon to perform this service, either by coming to Heidelberg himself or by preparing a written memorandum. Though Melanchthon was prepared to acknowledge several demands of the peasants as justified, he differed not a little from Luther in his judgment. In many respects he was more conservative than Luther. Since the peasants appealed to the gospel, he first held up to them the true doctrine. Christian faith is something other than force and coercion. Here is required the obedience which men owe to the government. As a humanist he strongly emphasized the natural law. Melanchthon stated the opinion that through the law the peasants were bound to their established burdens. Among them he even reckoned serfdom. While he called the peasants to obedience, he exhorted the lords to mildness. The first step should be church reforms, then social difficulties would gradually be worked out. But this counsel came too late. The land was already up in flames with the Peasants' War, and force had to decide the issue.

During the most violent days of the Peasants' War, which Luther viewed in the light of the Judgment Day, he determined to lay before the world a last confession. On June 13, 1525, he betrothed himself to Katherine von Bora, a refugee nun from the cloister at Nimbschen. Melanchthon, who had had no hint of this move, was dismayed by the news. To Luther's marriage he had no objections; it only appeared questionable to him whether the act was wisely timed. He emphasized, however, that his relation to Luther's doctrine remained unaffected, whether Luther had erred in his personal life or not. When, according to the custom of the time, Luther held the wedding celebration fourteen days later, Melanchthon was among the guests. Between the friends no alienation was caused by Luther's marriage. Afterward as well as before, Melanchthon was a frequent guest in Luther's house, even though their wives did not get along very well together.

The controversy between Erasmus and Luther over free will left a marked impression upon Melanchthon. Melanchthon, who regarded himself as a pupil of Erasmus, had tried ever since his arrival in Wittenberg to see to it that no antagonism should develop between Erasmus and the Wittenbergers. He had even induced Luther to write again to Erasmus, and to influence him to avoid a controversy. But Erasmus had already committed himself. He could not retreat. The treatise *On Free Will* had to appear. Although Melanchthon was no longer an Erasmian in the same sense as before, still he inevitably felt himself affected as a humanist. He himself desired that the unsettled questions between humanism and the Reformation might be discussed for once in competent fashion. Already in the summer of 1524 he had declared that on such an occasion the predestination of man and the question of personal freedom of decision should be treated. Now Erasmus had recognized and taken up this question as the most important of the unsettled problems. And Luther testified in his answer that Erasmus had hit the nail on the head. Here, indeed, lay the real core of the difference in views. Erasmus had informed Melanchthon of his intention. Melanchthon in his reply by no means dissociated himself from Luther, but declared himself in agreement with him, and promised a calm and objective rejoinder by Luther. The situation did not remain at this point. Both Luther and Erasmus contributed to the fact that the controversy became sharper and sharper. This Melanchthon regretted. Despite the break between Erasmus and Luther, however, Melanchthon for his part never cut off his correspondence with the once so admired master. He remained in touch with him until Erasmus' death.

Melanchthon did not continue to be a passive spectator in this controversy. In his memorial to Erasmus he later revealed that this dissension between Erasmus and Luther had deeply affected him. In his conception of man and of the freedom of the human will, however, he remained strongly influenced by Erasmus. In his inclination to draw sharp lines and in his effort to work pedagogically, he succeeded in combining the solution of an Erasmus with that of Luther. The doctrine of predestination was too obscure and too deeply surrounded by mystery for the simple man of the people to understand. Since Melanchthon's starting point was human experience, his view, for which he claimed the support of Rom. 2:14-15, had to leave room for a freedom of the will in the realm of " civil righteousness." For him, too, of course, everything in the inner life was traced back to God's immediate action. In this way much of the humanistic outlook was maintained and some features of Luther's views were attenuated.

In his commentary on the letter to the Colossians, which Melanchthon published in 1527, this mediating line is drawn. The two realms — civil existence and religious existence — must not be mingled. That is what the fanatics had attempted, and Melanchthon still had a vivid recollection of the controversies with Thomas Müntzer and with Karlstadt. Müntzer's letter to Melanchthon at Eastertime

68 MELANCHTHON

in 1524 had been clear enough. Henceforth he taught more fully about free will, and underscored its use in questions of outward righteousness. Here he approaches the question psychologically and retreats from his original theological position. Man has freedom to do good and avoid evil, but this freedom is hindered by the devil. "This is important to know, that the people may learn how weak and wretched a man he is who does not seek help from God." With Luther he did not part company over this teaching, yet there were pupils of Luther's who accused him of having turned to a view different from Luther's. Some regretted the polemic in the *Visitation Articles;* others took offense at the exposition of the doctrine of repentance and the necessity for the preaching of the law. John Agricola, in Eisleben, emphasized, on the contrary, that both repentance and faith come from the gospel; the law is annulled by the gospel — this, he insisted, was Luther's teaching. Melanchthon's view he saw as a defection from the doctrine of justification. Luther had to arbitrate. He found here a quarrel over words. At bottom it is a pedagogical question whether man is said to be led to repentance by fear of divine wrath or whether repentance arises from love of God and his righteousness. Melanchthon was vindicated when Luther declared that faith involves the conscience and must be included in repentance. So Luther also taught in his two catechisms.

Melanchthon might regard himself as awkward and impractical, but through the pressure of current events he was forced to turn his attention to practical tasks. If the Enthusiast movement in Wittenberg had caused him to occupy himself with questions of church order, he also had occasion later to take up the questions of education and of Christian moral standards.

9. THE PROMOTION OF STUDIES
AND THE CHURCH VISITATION

As Luther opposed the fanatics through preaching, Melanchthon attacked the acute problems in the realm of education. He held that better educational training would necessarily help the still evolving Evangelical Church to escape harm from irresponsible people. Above all, he was concerned about the school. As early as 1520, Melanchthon had set up a private school at his home. Its purpose was to give pupils a better preparation for the university than the ordinary Latin school provided. In addition, it was to supplement his originally meager income. Not only were the ancient languages thoroughly taught there, but also mathematics, Aristotelian physics, and ethics. Many of his best pupils went through this private school, and others worked there as teachers.

In Eisleben where Hermann Tulich and John Agricola rebuilt the Latin school, in Magdeburg where Nicholas von Amsdorf worked, and especially in Nuremberg, Melanchthon took part in setting up the classical school (*Gymnasium*). He attended the openings of each one. The Nurembergers would gladly have kept him for themselves, but Melanchthon recommended his best friend, Camerarius. Just at this time the promotion of studies lay especially on his heart.

Studies had suffered because of the unrest at Wittenberg. Students had gone elsewhere or had turned to practical professions. Luther and Melanchthon worked hand in hand to restore the prestige and importance of academic learning. While Luther advocated schools in his treatise *To the Councilmen*, 1524, Melanchthon from 1523 on energetically promoted the reform of studies at the university. The disputations, which had been neglected, were revived. Alongside them the Reformer placed the declamation, a rhetorical exercise that he valued just as highly as the disputation. In order to maintain them at high quality, prizes were established for the best authors of theses and the best respondents. To set examples, the teachers also had to deliver these addresses. Melanchthon himself was the most active in this realm, either speaking in person or preparing treatises which were delivered by others. The purpose of these exercises was to discipline students in logical thinking and acumen, but also secondarily to develop rhetorical style. Melanchthon also hoped in this way to be able to draw students into scientific work. While Monday, Tuesday, Thursday, and Friday were retained for lectures, Wednesday and Saturday were designated for disputations and declamations. What Melanchthon thought of the theological curriculum can be ascertained in detail from his *Reflection on the Study of Theology.*

In keeping with the foundations that he had laid for scientific knowledge, Melanchthon worked out statutes for the university and its faculties during the following years. He quickly made a name for himself as an experienced organizer in the academic realm, and was consulted in the founding of new universities such as Marburg and Königsberg, and called in to help with the reorganization of older schools including Tübingen, Leipzig, and Heidelberg.

From the beginning, Luther ungrudgingly acknowledged Melanchthon's academic superiority. In many respects he accepted guidance from him, especially in his linguistic studies, above all in Greek. Even the manner in which Melanchthon approached the exposition of the Bible influenced him greatly. That was more than Erasmus had offered. Master Philip possessed a special ability to state the decisive thing briefly and to find a striking formulation for it.

Luther was extremely eager to gain this man for the theological faculty. The prevailing regulations, which required possession of the degree of doctor of theology as a condition for acceptance into the theological faculty, were waived in his case. Though he was merely a master, he was, as Luther said, worth more than all the doctors. According to the university statutes, moreover, the rector should be an unmarried man. Melanchthon, who was elected to this office in 1524, was the first to be exempted from this requirement. His prestige in the university was incomparably great. As for the breadth and comprehensiveness of his knowledge, no man was his equal. Not only was he an expert on antiquity and theology, but there was no realm in which he did not possess extensive knowledge, from jurisprudence through mathematics and natural sciences to medicine. Melanchthon was regarded actually as a universal scholar. His textbooks were eagerly used, addresses based on his material were delivered, manuscripts of other authors were revised by him for the press. For all, he was the preceptor. With this title many expressed in a word what they owed to him.

The great reputation and trust that Melanchthon enjoyed in the learned world is disclosed also in the fact that numerous scholars requested him to add a foreword to their works. This was considered a special recommendation. Melanchthon also possessed the capacity to say something essential in a few pages. His forewords therefore are no less significant than his addresses and memoranda. To be sure, repetitions were unavoidable here when the same author was forced to write frequently about the same subject.

Melanchthon's own lectures were extremely versatile
and profound. Beside his obligatory philosophical lectures
and expositions of classical texts stand the interpretations
of Biblical books, among which his favorites were Romans,
Colossians, and the Proverbs of Solomon. In addition he
lectured at definite intervals on basic questions of theology,
on the basis of his *Loci.*

In the midst of the crisis of the Peasants' War, Frederick
the Wise died. While he lived he had frequently shown his
favor to Melanchthon. He knew what his university possessed in this scholar, and he had demonstrated his confidence in him during the Wittenberg uprisings and also
later. At the burial of the elector, Luther preached the sermon and Melanchthon had to deliver the memorial address. In contrast to Luther, who had never spoken to the
elector who had held his protecting hand over him, Melanchthon knew him from frequent visits. He was able,
therefore, aptly to describe his nature, his character, and
his manner of rule. Even the piety and the conservative nature of the elector he succeeded in setting in the proper
light. In the memorial address he also discussed Frederick's
attitude toward Luther and the Reformation, extolled him
for having dared to take the gospel under his protection,
and emphasized that for this act he ought never to be forgotten.

The same confidence the young scholar enjoyed with
Frederick's brother, John the Steadfast. The latter did everything to keep Melanchthon in Wittenberg. The professor had no more outward cares. The elector, however, also
involved him more deeply in the general problems of the
church, both in the establishment of general standards and
in decisions on individual cases. After the Peasants' War,
public opinion needed to be stabilized. Melanchthon represented an authoritarian outlook. This was connected with

his theological conviction that the government was a gift of God which served the maintenance of life, and to which for God's sake the Christian must be obedient. He condemned all rebellion, and justified the uncompromising action of the government in such cases as the Peasants' War.

Great confusion prevailed in all parts of the country. In these circumstances a thorough reorganization of the church's affairs had become all the more urgent. The proposal of a church visitation, which Luther's old friend Nicholas Hausmann had submitted to the elector as early as 1524, was taken up by Luther immediately after the uprising in Saxony was suppressed. It was necessary to bring order into the congregations. Though Luther had provided the foundation for public worship, there was a general lack of churchly authority that could have brought about a unified regulation of congregational life. Private opinions and arbitrariness frequently prevailed. It was therefore very significant that, in spite of the distress of the times, the elector in 1527 instituted a church and school visitation. The visitation commissions, which inquired into all individual offices, were to examine the clergy, regulate the administration of church property, and establish schools. Instructions for the examination of pastors were drawn up by Melanchthon. This Latin *Instruction* is his most characteristic work. He also took part in the visitation in Thuringia, and was able to learn at first hand what church affairs looked like. After the impressions and experiences of the visitation tours Melanchthon now compiled the *Instruction to the Visitors*, 1528. This work was examined by Luther and Bugenhagen, who suggested only a few changes, " for practically everything in it pleases us, since it is arranged in a most simple fashion for the people." Luther supplied a foreword for this writing on October 12,

1527. According to the instruction contained in it, the
Reformation was carried further into effect in Electoral
Saxony.

Of the 18 articles in the *Instruction to the Visitors* 14
deal with doctrine, the remainder with church order. Pastors are enjoined to preach the whole gospel, not only the
parts that suit individual tastes. Since law and gospel belong together, repentance and the fear of God must not be
forgotten. The simple man must always be kept in mind,
sermons are to be made comprehensible through examples,
but above all, emphasis is to be laid on the Christian life.
The problem is to overcome the results of fanatical errors.
In all this the government has the duty of promoting the
preaching of the gospel. Worship is to be held daily. On
Sunday, Wednesday, and Friday there is preaching; on
other days, the morning lection is taken from the New
Testament and the evening lection from the Old. On Sunday afternoon, when the servants and the young people
come to church, the Ten Commandments, the Creed, and
the Lord's Prayer are expounded. Melanchthon also remembered the schoolmasters, for whom he developed a
course for the instruction of children. In this way he provided essential building stones for the reconstruction of
the Evangelical church.

The difficult visitation tours were of great importance
for Melanchthon. Now he saw what the conditions were in
the church. The ignorance that he encountered seemed
boundless; the errors he met had to be clarified and refuted. His concern here was positive instruction; to a lesser
degree, polemic. This is the reason why the " Visitation
Articles " are so simply and clearly composed. It had become clear to Melanchthon that a beginning cannot be
made with the gospel, with the word of grace, where men
have experienced nothing of God in their inmost souls and

have not yet shown the fruits of repentance. He had to accommodate himself to the defective understanding of the people, who so often misunderstood the doctrine of justification. Repentance, he said at this time, must precede faith; the law must first produce fear and contrition in a man. If he had earlier placed first the grace that accomplishes all things, now he noted the necessity also of conceding to the human will a place of its own.

During the years of the visitation Melanchthon also occupied himself profoundly with catechetical problems. It was no completely new field for him. Already in 1523 and 1524 he had composed for his private pupils a little handbook that contained, besides the Decalogue, the Lord's Prayer, and the Creed, also an alphabet, sayings of the seven sages, and numerous prayers that after the manner of the ancient church strongly emphasized the praise of God in his creation. Melanchthon devoted his interest not exclusively to the Latin school, however, but engaged himself likewise with questions of the elementary school, and wrote textbooks for it. Since Justus Jonas and John Agricola had not completed their catechisms, Melanchthon at Spalatin's wish composed a *Brief Exposition of the Ten Commandments, the Lord's Prayer, and the Creed* in 1527, even before Luther took up the same task. At the same time he also compiled *Several Sayings,* which contains the Biblical material for catechetical instruction. Later these sayings were reprinted frequently, which demonstrates their practical usefulness. As a book of sayings, however, it did not exercise a wide influence. The reason perhaps lies in the fact that Melanchthon diverged from the text of the Luther Bible and at places offered his own translations. In the next year he also gathered catechetical material for his own children, for use in his home. Obviously he was not completely satisfied with Luther's *Small Catechism.*

V

On the Political Stage

10. SPEYER AND MARBURG, 1529

Not only the reorganization of the church in Saxony but also other critical tasks devolved upon Melanchthon in this period. Even before the first imperial diet at Speyer he had had to furnish the elector with legal memoranda vindicating the new doctrine. Melanchthon, like Luther, was sure beyond doubt that the princes had the right to reform their territories. Since the political situation in 1526 was favorable to the Evangelical estates, they obtained a recess that secured the public peace. Within a year a church council was to open on German soil. In the meantime every estate should " so conduct itself and govern, as it hopes and trusts to answer to God and His Imperial Majesty." Not until two years later was the emperor once more in a position to take more decisive action upon current affairs. When a second diet at Speyer was convoked in 1529, there was a foreboding of evil in Germany. Melanchthon, who ascribed great importance to the position of the stars, thought that they foretold evil. He had to travel to the diet with the elector. The opening of negotiations made him still more uneasy. To his friend Camerarius he reported on March 15, 1529: " Today the imperial mandate was read. It is absolutely frightening. . . . Nevertheless, I hope that Christ will frustrate the counsel of those who want war." Melanchthon sought in his own way to influence the course of events. To Archduke Ferdinand, who presided at the diet, he dedicated a tract in the form of a preface to his commentary on Daniel. In this address he wrote that an ecclesiastical schism could not be removed by force. Only if the true Christian doctrine was proclaimed, could peace prevail. Melanchthon therefore begged the emperor's brother to see to it that the disputed issues were thoroughly discussed. It was only right to hear the other side. If a synod was not possible, then a smaller circle of upright men should be called together to discuss the pending questions. For the glory of God, Ferdinand must devote himself to restore the unity of the church through the purification of doctrine. This was a task worthy of a king. Melanchthon appended a Latin poem in which Germany appeared in lamentation and implored not only protection against the Turks but also peace in the church.

Meanwhile, a committee had prepared a resolution for the diet that would forbid every ecclesiastical innovation pending a council. No one dared be hindered from celebrating Mass; on the contrary, doctrinal opinions directed against the Mass were declared inadmissible. This last point affected primarily the Upper Germans. It was well known that the Evangelical estates would be split. While the Saxons were inclined to abandon the Swiss, Landgrave Philip and the representatives of the Upper German cities combated this attitude with great vigor. When the diet on April 19 elevated the proposed articles to an official resolution, the Evangelical minority had no recourse but to protest. In their now-famous *Protestation* they said: " In matters affecting the glory of God and the salvation of our souls, everyone must stand on his own before God and give account." They resolved, therefore, " to persevere with the grace and help of God in insisting that only God's Word and the holy gospel shall be purely preached, and nothing contrary to it."

This *Protestation* was the first concerted act of the Evangelical estates. Melanchthon had no part in its composition. He was deeply shocked and asked himself whether more should not be conceded to the emperor. He was so remote from reality that he still believed in the goodwill of the emperor. The danger that confronted the Evangelical estates caused them to unite. Saxony and Hesse entered into an alliance with the Upper German free cities, Strassburg, Nuremberg, and Ulm. Although the landgrave wished to include the Swiss in this alliance, Melanchthon was opposed to this plan. When his friend Oecolampadius wrote to him at Speyer urging him to use his influence in order that the Swiss would not be condemned unheard as " Sacramentarians," he published an open letter to Oecolampadius on the subject of the Lord's Supper. Though he had kept aloof from the controversy between Luther and Zwingli during the previous years, he expressed himself unambiguously here for the Lutheran conception. In agreement with Holy Scripture he wished to see the true presence of Christ in the Lord's Supper. Here it was a question of believing in the miracle, for " where heavenly things are concerned, one's judgment must be formed according to God's Word and not according to geometry." In this view he stood in sharp opposition to the Zwinglians. " For I could not appear," he wrote further, " as an author or defender of a new dogma." He suffered over the differences of opinion concerning the Lord's Supper. However, he had freed himself not only from the Scholastic tradition but also from the views of his friends, including Erasmus. He saw the latter's influence upon Zwingli with all clarity. In

his conception of Scripture, Melanchthon supported himself also by the authority of the church fathers, who had
come to assume great importance for him. In secret he
nourished the hope that the union of the various schools
of thought might be achieved on the basis of the ancient
church. His tract to Archduke Ferdinand hinted at this.
Both writings bear the same date. Though he wrote to
Oecolampadius that a conference of a few well-intentioned
men would further the cause of unity, he warned against
relying too much on one's own reason in questions of
faith. When the landgrave, proceeding from the conviction
that a political alliance would be sound only if it rested on
the basis of an agreement in ecclesiastical questions, returned to this concrete proposal in the summer of 1529
and issued the invitation for a religious colloquy at Marburg, however, Melanchthon had strong misgivings. With
Oecolampadius and others he was willing to discuss the
Sacrament; to treat the subject with Zwingli he considered
unfruitful. Nevertheless, along with Luther, he promised
to participate at Marburg.

On the first of October, 1529, Melanchthon engaged
Zwingli in a separate colloquy at Marburg. Though they
succeeded in reaching an understanding on certain preliminary questions, an agreement in the matter of the Lord's
Supper was not attained.

Zwingli made some notes in his presence. To them Melanchthon occasionally contributed his formulation. The
topics discussed first were Word and Spirit, for Melanchthon suspected Zwingli of spiritualism. Here they were
soon in accord, and likewise on the question of original sin.
However, when they came to the question of the Lord's
Supper, agreement could be established only on certain
preliminaries: that eating is equivalent to faith, i.e., " spiritual manducation." While Melanchthon spoke in Luther's

fashion of the miracle in the Supper, Zwingli rejected this conception. The two understood Scripture differently. In the interpretation of Eph. 4:10 they diverged. The fourth point discussed was Christology. Melanchthon surrendered the authority of Augustine and conceded that many of these witnesses supported Zwingli's view better. They did not reach the end, however. In the meantime night had fallen. The preliminary colloquy had not yielded much, nor had Luther's discussion with Oecolampadius; however, many misunderstandings were removed.

In the face of his previous attitude, Melanchthon was by no means ready for reconciliation or accommodation. He supported Luther's conception and spoke of a mysterious unification with the Savior in the Lord's Supper. He deliberately emphasized his independence in this conception. Hence the conversation, which had lasted six hours, led to no result. Melanchthon did not participate much in the colloquy on the following days. He thought he recognized that the Swiss proceeded from philosophical presuppositions which they imported into the questions of faith. The opponents, however, were full of mistrust toward him. They thought that he would hinder Luther from accommodating himself to them and would allow no agreement to be reached.

Here he left it to Luther to be the spokesman. Luther rejected the argument that related John 6:63 to the Supper. It was a gift if one could believe that Christ was bodily present in the bread. The paradox of " the hidden God " was a great and important matter to him. Luther shoved patristic authorities aside. For him the Word was decisive; he was captive to the Word. What God commanded must be done without prying speculation. This was the " humble mind."

Although Luther called upon Melanchthon: " Philip, you speak now, I am really exhausted," the preceptor did not allow himself to warm up to the subject. He maintained an altogether reserved manner. Even in the discussion of the Christological questions Zwingli disputed only with Luther. Not until the end of the colloquy was a union proposal made, which perhaps originated with Melanchthon. He was supposed to have conferred with Hedio, but finally to have influenced Luther against reconciliation, since he had other church-political intentions. The fifteen Marburg Articles presented a concord, indeed, but only a partially achieved concord.

Hedio reported, it is true, that Melanchthon had promised to work for an agreement. When Philip published his *Opinions of Several Ancient Authors Regarding the Lord's Supper* a year later, as an answer to Oecolampadius' polemic, he added a declaration on his own part: " I cannot believe otherwise than that Christ is truly present in the Sacrament; I know no reason why he should not be. The Sacraments are instituted as divine means to arouse our spirit to faith, and not merely as a sign to distinguish us Christians from the heathen. To avert controversy and offense one needs only to keep simply and without speculation to the words of Scripture." On the other hand, if one insisted on understanding everything, one turned Christianity into a philosophy.

When the clouds gathered ever more thickly on the political horizon, the elector of Saxony inquired of his theologians whether it was appropriate for Christians to resist the emperor. Melanchthon thought that resistance was contrary to God's commandment. The Christian must not revolt, but obey and endure. Even if the emperor did not keep his promises, his subjects would have no right to

rise against him. Those who urged resistance, such as the
Upper German cities, did not take the gospel seriously.
This was Melanchthon's honest conviction, and he considered himself obliged to use all his influence on its behalf.

Even before this question was clarified among the Wittenberg theologians, they were informed by the elector
that the emperor had announced a new diet. Now they had
to express their view on what should be said about the
doctrinal articles in dissension, and how far the Evangelical
estates could go in negotiations over them. The elector
made this order urgent. The theologians were to put aside
all other work and take up the articles that were necessary for the diet. Preliminary discussions were conducted
in the electoral residence at Torgau. At Melanchthon's
suggestion the articles in which nothing could be yielded
were first collected. These included the Lord's Supper in
both forms, the marriage of the clergy, the rejection of
private Masses, monasteries, and the oath due to the
bishop. Further articles over which negotiation was possible were compiled. They were put into mild and definite
words, without forsaking principle. To be sure, satisfaction had not yet been given to the imperial proclamation.
Melanchthon therefore was commissioned to bring the
statement of doctrine into proper form. Thus he was confronted with an enormous task, which was to prove of substantial importance for all Evangelical Christendom.

11. The Augsburg Confession
and Self-assertion

Since Luther was unable to appear in Augsburg at the
diet on account of the imperial ban, the decisive role there

fell to Melanchthon. He had already proved himself as theological adviser to the elector. It was to be anticipated, however, that now in the face of the approaching crisis a far greater and more important responsibility would devolve upon him. The Saxon theologians had completed certain preparatory tasks for their confession, but in Augsburg the greatest work still lay ahead. Here Melanchthon first became acquainted with Eck's *404 Theses* against Luther, which prompted Philip to point out the agreement of the Lutheran Church with the ancient church. Already at the end of the Torgau Articles, which had been composed before the journey to Augsburg, it was stated that positive doctrinal articles also might be set forth. As such, the Schwabach Articles were subjoined. Melanchthon now set himself to summarize the articles of faith in all brevity, while the Torgau Articles concerning abrogated abuses were moved to the second place. On May 11, 1530, the confession was finished and could be sent to Luther at the Coburg for his comments. Luther's verdict, which he returned with Melanchthon's work, is well known. No criticism of content was intended when he said it pleased him very well, and he did not know how he could improve or change anything, nor would it be fitting to do so. The underlying reason followed in the words: " For I cannot tread so softly and gently." In any case, Luther cherished the wish: " Christ our Lord help that it may bring forth great and good fruits, as we hope and pray. Amen! " In the following six weeks before the presentation of the Augsburg Confession, Melanchthon imperturbably polished it. His preface was withdrawn and replaced by one composed by Chancellor Gregory Brück. In the chapter room of the bishop's palace, then, on June 25, 1530, the Augsburg Confession was read in the German language by the Saxon

Vice-Chancellor, Dr. Christian Beyer, so loudly and distinctly that the crowd standing outside — estimated at three thousand — heard every word. The reading lasted two hours. The emperor acted bored or slept.

Luther was just as clearly aware of the greatness of this hour as were the eyewitnesses. He expressed his joy that Christ was glorified at the imperial diet by this " most beautiful confession." Melanchthon later became despondent and had to be strengthened again by Luther through the strong faith of his letters. Luther, however, never reproached him for having composed a " gentle stepper." He saw in the confession a testimony of faith born of the hour, and for it he was thankful.

Although others collaborated on the Augsburg Confession, it is Melanchthon's work. He himself regarded it throughout his life as his intellectual property and did not hesitate to alter and improve it, both before the first printing and at every later edition. Though Melanchthon had inserted his special views, the Augsburg Confession was the product of one mold, bearing the stamp of the Lutheran spirit. Its merits are obvious: if it was precise in expression, it was at the same time also easily understandable. In this regard it remains Melanchthon's masterpiece.

In great calm and sobriety the individual questions of faith are discussed in 28 articles and illuminated from the standpoint of the doctrine of justification. Thus Articles 1 to 6 treat the saving work of God, and Articles 7 to 17 the church and the means of grace, to the return of Christ. Four miscellaneous articles follow, in which Melanchthon expresses himself in a way different from his previous manner: on free will, the cause of sin, good works, and the invocation of saints. Then came the second part with its 7 articles on abuses. Doctrine must be consonant with the ancient church, therefore it need not always be contrary to the Roman teaching. Where agreement cannot be reached, however, it must be made clear that God is to be obeyed rather than men.

Here, Melanchthon did not adhere exactly to Luther's manner of teaching. Whether in the doctrine of justification, of free will, or even the article on the Lord's Supper, the formulations were his own. This right he claimed for himself, and Luther conceded it to him. It cannot be asserted, on the other hand, that Melanchthon presented his subjective opinions in the confession. It was the common faith of the Reformation, brought into a definite form, which was to remain for centuries the standard expression of the Evangelical faith. Melanchthon was convinced that the Reformation signified nothing else than a new apprehension of the ancient gospel and hence a purification of doctrine from all dross, from human precepts and authorities. Luther himself, on June 20, had protested against the idea that *his* personal views should be presented, as if he were the issue and as if he had imposed his conception upon others. For him the issue was solely the truth.

The effect of this confession was great upon both friend and foe. Spalatin, conscious of the way it was being received, wrote: " On this day action was taken on one of the greatest works that ever took place on earth."

All the more indignant were many at the diet when they saw how despondent Melanchthon was. Even to Luther his condition remained no secret, so that the latter had to write to him: " If we are in error, then we must retract; but if we fight for the truth, why should we doubt the promises of him who said, ' Cast your cares upon me '? " It was unjust, however, when he sought the cause of this anxiety in Melanchthon's ambition, and thought, " Philip should not make himself God and be so concerned about himself." Philip thought about himself least of all. But he had constructed a false picture of the situation. Above all, Melanchthon had a boundless confidence in the emperor, as Luther had also had in the days of the Diet at Worms. He saw Charles V in the light of clemency and of peace. In him he saw one of the ideal figures depicted by the classical authors.

As an amateur in political affairs, Melanchthon was not the right man to find the proper path among the promises and threats that surrounded him. Always he feared that the Evangelical estates would become ensnared, and at this point he himself was the first to make concessions. Luther wrote to him: " You are not anxious about your life, but you fear for the common cause. . . . Full of confidence, I observe outward things, and care nothing about those threatening and raging papists. If we are ruined, Christ also is ruined — he, the ruler of the world! If that happens, I would rather fall with Christ than stand with the emperor."

With his peaceful temperament, however, Melanchthon wished to leave no stone unturned to attain union with the opponents. He begged the elector first to press only for the Lord's Supper in both forms and for clerical marriage. In all other points ways for concord would be found. The elector gave him permission also to negotiate over these matters with representatives of the opposition.

The discussions into which Melanchthon was drawn in Augsburg by the imperial and papal side saw a compliant man who intended to hold out merely for a minimum — clerical marriage and abolition of the Mass.

When the representatives of the old faith on August 3 had presented their *Confutation of the Augsburg Con-*

fession and the comparison of doctrine was discussed in the committee, Melanchthon again showed his yielding disposition. The more harshly he rejected a reconciliation with the Swiss, the more compliant he was toward the old believers. Melanchthon the mediator was ready even to water down the Augsburg Confession, but the estates did not permit it. Hence several of the princes of the church — the Cardinal of Salzburg no less than the Bishop of Augsburg and the papal legate himself — tried to draw him into further concessions. He was often reproached for his letter to Campeggio, in which Melanchthon wrote: " In doctrine we agree with the true catholic church. The false teachers we ourselves have fought; we are ready to obey the Roman Church, insofar as we are permitted to abolish all abuses in practice." Later he also adjured the legate to work for peace. In his effort to be in agreement with the universal church he thought he was giving up nothing in his own faith. In the Roman system he saw innovations that had to be abolished if unity were to be achieved with the ancient teachers of the church and the ancient councils.

After the unexpected departure of Landgrave Philip on August 6, when the unity conversations were elevated to an instrument of imperial politics, Melanchthon became a central figure in the negotiations. In his discussions with Eck he actually thought that the opposition would object to the new doctrine only on formal grounds. Hence he was also prepared to renounce the *sola fide* if only it were granted to him that he taught rightly on the righteousness of faith. The heart must reach its own conclusion that God forgives its sin for Christ's sake, as the church fathers and Thomas Aquinas had also taught. To Eck's Thomistic conception, Melanchthon thus had only to add " that a terrified conscience and true faith are necessary for for

giveness." Although Melanchthon intended to yield here,
and a union formula was found in: " We become righteous
through grace *and* faith," the difficulty broke out again
along the lines of ecclesiastical ordinances: clerical marriage, the cup for the laity, and private Mass. Even in a
subcommittee in which Melanchthon took part, however,
no progress was made. The negotiations shattered on the
emperor's demand that the Mass had to be retained.

Melanchthon was in complete consternation. He had a
foreboding of dreadful times to come and foresaw the ruin
of Germany. Was Luther right when he wrote to him that
he had allowed himself to be guided too much by his
philosophy? Had he allowed his actions in the political
negotiations to be determined not so much by faith as by
" real facts "? Luther was well informed about events at
Augsburg and had adequate grounds for a sharp judgment. Therefore he urged Melanchthon not to act as if
everything depended on his insight. The envoys of the
Evangelical cities were already considerably angered
against him. The Nuremberger Jerome Baumgartner complained bitterly over his procedure and his constant concessions.

Melanchthon realized not only that he had lost the
favor of the landgrave but also that the people were no
longer well disposed toward him. To Matthew Alber in
Reutlingen he wrote on August 25: " I know that our
moderation is reproached by the people. It is not fitting,
however, to heed the cry of the masses; we must look to
peace and the future. If concord can be restored in Germany, it will be a great blessing for all."

The various negotiations in Augsburg, meanwhile, had
finally shown Melanchthon that an agreement was not to
be expected and that the opposition, despite all its fair

words, had no such intention. Beyond certain external usages the opposition would yield nothing. The divergent standpoints became ever clearer and showed that in a series of basic articles an agreement was impossible.

Under these circumstances it was understandable that in September, Melanchthon decided to expound in greater detail the basic Evangelical articles of faith which were attacked in the *Confutation,* and to demonstrate their truth from Scripture. He acted here not on his own responsibility but on order of the estates. Now he thought no more of conciliation, but exposed the contrasts emphatically. The emperor, it is true, had refused a copy of the *Confutation* to the Evangelicals, but Camerarius had copied down so much of it during its reading that Melanchthon could make reference to it. When on September 22 the draft of the recess, in which the emperor declared the Evangelicals refuted, was made known, the Saxon Chancellor Dr. Brück submitted Melanchthon's *Apology.* On the same day the elector left Augsburg, accompanied by Spalatin and Melanchthon.

During the journey Melanchthon worked further on his *Apology.* At home he revised it at his leisure, preparing to send it together with the Augsburg Confession to the printer. The situation unexpectedly suffered a long delay, however, so that the edition was not ready until April or early May of the next year. It contained only the Latin text. The *Apology* held close to the structure of the Augsburg Confession. It contained a theological undergirding of the confession, except that it was more freely and sharply conceived than the latter. Justus Jonas undertook the German version of the *Apology.* It was designed in a more pedagogical form.

The *Apology* universally received a favorable reception

on the Evangelical side. Although Melanchthon characterized it as a private work, it soon took its place alongside
the Augsburg Confession as a confessional document of the
Evangelical estates, with which it was published in 1531.

As Melanchthon had already taken justifying faith in
Luther's sense as his point of departure in the Augsburg
Confession, and had developed all further questions of
faith from it, he did the same in the *Apology*. Faith in
Christ, which justifies the sinner before God, provides its
inner structure. He managed to leave aside all abstract
formulations of questions and to concentrate only on the
essential. In this sense Melanchthon is thoroughly practical: he emphasizes that by which the heart may be
quieted; his concern is to have sure ground under his feet
and to attain to full assurance. For this reason he has no
use for formalistic conceptions. The whole document is
quietly and soberly written, and yet the reader senses the
trembling heart of the author who has experienced in himself that about which he writes, and therefore can present
his view with complete positiveness and assurance. Not re-
sentment that his efforts at mediation have been rejected,
but the necessity to express himself more comprehensibly
than was possible in the brief setting of the Augsburg Confession, is the reason why Melanchthon here set forth the
Lutheran standpoint more firmly than he had done in
Augsburg. Ignoring the Confutators, for whom he has only
disdain, he gets down to business immediately.

Melanchthon reaches back to Scripture and experience.
He expounds the impotence of man, his resistance to God's
Word, and his trust in his own power. From this situation
of the natural man, the result of original sin, he comes to
" the supreme article of the entire Christian doctrine,
which alone shows the way to a clear understanding of

Holy Scripture and to a right knowledge of Christ." Thus from the first, Melanchthon has understood the letter to the Romans as the key to Scripture, and has brought the Evangelical approach to clear expression. In order to love God one must pass through the new birth and accept the benefits of Christ. Here no one can do anything for the other; everyone must hear for himself that Christ has died for him. This faith is no assent but a trust in God's mercy in Christ and a reliance upon it. This faith alone lets man become righteous before God. Out of the sinner comes a righteous man. These are no mere words or formulas. As the feeling of sin is no idle thing, so forgiveness is no weak comfort. If a share were ascribed to human achievement, it would mean " laying Christ again into the grave." These words are no slip of Paul's pen, but, rather, his basic attitude, that everything which man does by his own power is merely sin before God. God accepts man not because of works but out of pure grace, for Christ's sake.

Melanchthon avoids writing about predestination in this context. He holds to the view, which Luther also advocated later, that this doctrine can confuse simple souls. In a letter to John Brentz he explains his procedure: " I teach that men become acceptable to God for Christ's sake, i.e., righteous through faith. To this is then added the fulfillment of the laws, which is promised as its reward. Righteousness at the same time has eternal life, for which reason faith alone gives life, in that it gives the heart peace. This is simple and easily understood."

Melanchthon realizes that the church is " no Platonic ' republic.' " To the visible church belong only a few characteristic marks: the right preaching of the Word, the right administration of the Sacraments. Melanchthon does not develop this point of doctrine in detail, because he does not

wish to widen the breach. According to his view, absolu-
tion, ordination to the office of preaching, prayer, and
many other ordinances could be called sacraments. The
main point is not what they are called but whether they are
rightly used. After the *Confutation* it was necessary also to
formulate more precisely the Evangelical view regarding
Roman abuses. As he says in the Preface that the holy
word of the gospel dare not be denied or rejected, even if
still greater danger and resistance are experienced as a result, so he expands this conception throughout the *Apology*. The cause itself he would commit to God.

In many respects the Augsburg Diet had opened the participants' eyes to the state of affairs. Fearing that war might
break out, Melanchthon incessantly sought to promote
unity and thus to assure peace. After the founding of the
Smalcald League, indeed, he became apprehensive that political interests might be mingled with the innermost concerns of religion and confuse it. Though he had yielded in
the question of the right of resistance against the emperor,
he did not wish to have religion protected by political
means. Hence we see Melanchthon in the 1530's continu-
ing his activity for a union, both on the Evangelical side
and further through negotiations with Catholics.

12. Paths and Efforts of His Own

Melanchthon did not reach maturity as a theologian all
at once. His *Loci* of 1521 were the deposit of his youthful
ideas of faith, as they had first emerged in his encounter
with Luther. In the following years he had undergone a
further development and had adopted and adapted stimulations from various sides. The encounter with the fanatics,
Luther's controversy with Erasmus, the church visitations,

and the diet at Augsburg with the subsequent union negotiations had not left him unaffected. In his comments on
the epistle to the Colossians it came to light that he now
preferred the doctrine of man as his point of departure in
theology, wishing to remove predestination from that position. In his Romans commentary of 1532 also he emphasized this conception, which he regarded as the Pauline
view. Amid his many activities Melanchthon had devoted
himself to a new edition of his *Loci,* which he published
in 1535. By 1541 it had undergone six printings. Of course
he took Scripture alone as his foundation, but he also
wished to hear the judgment of the universal church. Out
of the variety of existing conceptions the church needed a
clear teaching. To set this forth in all purity, letting it appear without polemic, was his aim. In every section of his
textbook he first presented witnesses from Scripture, then
he also appended those of the church fathers. Melanchthon
now considered it necessary to call attention more emphatically to the free will of man. " God draws men, but
he draws only willing men ": this word of Chrysostom's had
long impressed him and induced him to emphasize man's
decision, which later was reproached as synergism.

In the *Instruction to the Visitors,* Melanchthon had explained that in the last analysis the all-important thing is
the preaching of repentance and forgiveness. Whoever
neglects this and pursues unnecessary questions instead
will, according to I Tim. 1:19, suffer shipwreck of his
faith. For the same reasons, he thinks, Paul has played
down the question of predestination. One must hold not
to a hidden decree of God but to the redemption which has
come through Christ. Justification takes place, moreover,
only where one consciously grasps the salvation offered him
in Christ. Therefore, Melanchthon does not speak of the

passivity of man. The human will must not be idle, but must resist weakness and sin. True, it is necessary to extol the grace of God, which he grants to men through his mercy, yet men must also be admonished not to become secure and sluggish.

The newly revised *Loci* of 1535 still does not present a systematic work that connects the individual parts into a unity. Here, for the most part, the sections are only placed one after another. This is due not only to Melanchthon's personal inclination, but also to his intention of composing a textbook that will be as lucid as possible. In comparison with his earlier expositions, to which incidentally he nowhere refers, much appears narrower here, but much also seems deepened. He sets the objective aspect of the faith more in the foreground, assigning to the subjective side a secondary place. Like the Augsburg Confession, this book also was designed to furnish proof that Evangelical Christianity stood in continuity with the ancient church. Although Melanchthon in 1521 still considered it necessary to bypass the ancient church doctrines, his encounter with John Campanus, the publication of the anti-Trinitarian treatise of Michael Servetus, and finally the fight with the Baptists confronted him with the necessity of expounding in detail the doctrine of the Trinity and Christology. Of course, he emphasizes here too that the right knowledge of God is given in the gospel of Christ. As he has already done on earlier occasions, he devotes his attention here also to the natural and the divine law. He hints that even after the Fall man retains an awareness that his origin is from God. In order to be brought onto God's path, to be sure, he needs conversion. This is accomplished in him by God's Word, the Holy Spirit, and the will of man himself, who cannot be idle. Melanchthon omits the discussion of the origin of sin. To bring it into connection with God's fore-knowledge appeared to him blasphemous. When he treats the salvation of man, his interest lies in the forgiveness of sins for Christ's sake. This he identifies with justification. If man is sure of forgiveness, his heart is grasped by the Holy Spirit and ready for obedience.

Melanchthon now concentrated in particular on the concept of the church. According to his view the church has been in existence from the beginning, even though it was represented by few men. He distinguishes four ages of the church: the age of Christ and the apostles; the age of Origen, in which Neoplatonism and Christianity became connected; the age of Augustine, with his deepening of the faith; and finally, the age of secularization during the dark Middle Ages. In this sketch of church history Luther also found his place. With great penetration, Melanchthon portrays the work of the Reformer, who has set the divine light once more on its lampstand. In the church everything depends now on pure doctrine. This must be taught and preached. It is the genuine mark identifying Christians. Melanchthon has no hesitation in describing the church as an institution of learning or a school. He sees running through the church a chain of tradition that is formed by those who teach the pure gospel. In comparison with Luther, an intellectualistic trait is noticeable in Melanchthon's books. Much sounds directly Scholastic. But that is not the essential. His basic conception has remained unchanged; only particular points of doctrine have been expanded and worked out in comparison with older presentations.

The forthcoming religious colloquies forced him to attain clarity in the question of tradition. The church stands under its head, Christ, and is first and foremost bound to

the Word. It also has to heed the testimony of its members,
however, and since it works through men, it is subjected to
external influences. Nevertheless, it remains the church of
the truth if it has the Word on its side. To this extent it
depends internally more on consensus with the Word than
on consensus with external authority.

Conversations that Melanchthon had had with English
bishops in Wittenberg had not remained without influence
upon him. They had brought to his attention the relative
value of tradition. Thus in the *Wittenberg Articles,* Article
10, he had pointed out that every Christian has freedom,
but that in view of tradition we " must deal discreetly "
with Christian freedom.

Although the *Loci* of 1535 otherwise agrees with the
teaching of the Augsburg Confession and the *Apology,* a
change is already noticeable in the doctrine of the Lord's
Supper. Melanchthon always maintained that in this respect also he represented the views of the ancient church.
Oecolampadius had convinced him, however, that even in
the ancient period there were two different conceptions of
the Supper. After this, Melanchthon took pains to teach
more cautiously about the Supper. His conferences with
Martin Bucer in Kassel also were not without importance
for him in this connection. Thus in treating the doctrine
of the Supper in the *Loci* he spoke only of the spiritual
presence of Christ and of inner communion with him. Of
the connection of Christ with the elements, he said nothing
further. He had no desire to initiate disputations over
these questions.

Luther no doubt had seen that Melanchthon was going
his own way. For friendship's sake he remained silent. It
is almost incomprehensible how Luther could do that. In
view of his great trust in Melanchthon he obviously re-

garded these divergences as not too weighty. For this reason, however, some of Luther's pupils attacked Melanchthon all the more vehemently. Did Melanchthon mean to
impute value to man's activity over against God, in the
Erasmian sense? Should Luther's doctrine of justification
be endangered by him? Luther paid no further attention to
the accusations, but Conrad Cordatus denounced him for
having shifted closer to the Catholic view. To this misunderstanding Melanchthon himself had given occasion when
he attempted to explain justification more clearly for
simple Christians and spoke of repentance as the condition
of justification. Melanchthon received news of these attacks while he was in Württemberg to help with the university reform at Tübingen. He directed a letter to the
Wittenberg professors in which he explained the situation.
" I know that Luther thinks as I do," he wrote, " but certain ignorant men cling to his strong expressions without
asking whither they lead. I do not wish to fight with them."
Luther, too, wished that all controversy could be avoided.
But Cordatus was not the only assailant. The Freiberg
preacher Jacob Schenk was another. From the elector came
an inquiry; he had Chancellor Brück confer with Luther
and Bugenhagen. Apparently Luther calmed the elector
and induced him not to pursue the matter any further.

For Melanchthon, however, it was a bitter experience
that some of his own pupils turned against him and accused him of heresy. In later years, too, he frequently found
it his lot that ungrateful pupils assailed him. He gave expression to his mood in an address " On the Ingratitude of
the Cuckoo." In these years he became more lonely. His relation with Luther was strained. Petty spirits attacked him
out of envy or injured ambition. Thus it is understandable
that a vexatious mood developed in him, and he spoke of

the bondage in which he had to live. In spite of this depression of spirit, however, Melanchthon remained gratefully attached to Luther. Their personal relation was not
interrupted. Perhaps it was their common opposition to
Agricola that drove them closer together again. The latter
had renewed the controversy over the preaching of the law,
which he had begun ten years before. He repeated his
teaching that the gospel alone leads man to conversion and
that the law is completely superfluous. Luther was enraged, issued him a strong reprimand, and demanded a
public retraction. Agricola acquiesced, but left Wittenberg
secretly and went to Berlin. Deep inside he nourished a
grudge against Luther and Melanchthon.

Master Philip fell into a similar tension with Andrew
Osiander during these years. Much as he agreed with the
influential Nuremberg preacher, he did not entirely share
his views of justification and confession. Since he criticized
Osiander's procedure and admonished him to peace, there
arose an aversion between them which in later years was
to break out into violent controversy.

The theological opposition between Wittenberg and
Upper Germany was destined to show itself powerfully
once more in the 1540's. When the Archbishop of Cologne,
Hermann von Wied, trusting in the recess of Regensburg
(Ratisbon), 1541, intended to introduce the Reformation
in his archdiocese, he summoned Bucer and Melanchthon
to Bonn. To the *Cologne Reformation,* a document that
in the main stems from Bucer, Melanchthon contributed
several sections. The draft was thoroughly discussed with
the archbishop before it was presented to the territorial
diet.

On the question of the Lord's Supper, Melanchthon had
assumed a different position. In Frankfurt he had discussed

the matter with Calvin. In the new edition of the Augsburg Confession, 1540, the wording of the tenth article was greatly altered. The principle that the body and blood of Christ are truly present in the Supper was omitted. Instead, it was merely affirmed that with the bread and wine in the Supper the body and blood of Christ were offered. This new formula unleashed great controversies. Melanchthon had seen no need to oppose Bucer's formulation of the doctrine of the Supper in the *Cologne Reformation*. Only when the document appeared in print was it noticed that here the Sacrament was characterized as a work of faith. Amsdorf immediately reported this to Luther, who showed such great dissatisfaction over this formula that Melanchthon thought he would be obliged to leave Wittenberg. Luther smelled fanaticism again. His verdict of the article on the Lord's Supper in this book was therefore rather sharp: " And everything is too long, a great babbling; I surely smell that chatterbox Bucer in it."

Melanchthon was unhappy that a new Eucharistic controversy threatened to break out. The serious political situation permitted no new theological fights. " Our adversaries raise their heads, and we tear ourselves apart," he declared in deep depression. Early in October, 1544, meanwhile, appeared Luther's writing, *Brief Confession of the Holy Sacrament Against the Fanatics*. It was more moderate than had been feared and expected in Wittenberg. Bucer and Melanchthon were not mentioned. To be sure, the elector himself had requested Luther not to write against Melanchthon. Otherwise, Luther's treatise was by no means gentle. It described all who held a different view of the Supper as " bedeviled." Now Melanchthon carefully avoided expressing himself further on this theme, though Calvin besieged him to show his colors.

VI

Union Efforts

13. CONCILIATION ATTEMPTS AND BROAD CONTACTS

While still on the way from Torgau to Augsburg, Melanchthon wrote to Bishop Cricius of Plock, who had invited him to Poland, that " burdensome affairs " now required him to take up questions that basically did not interest him. Only reluctantly had Melanchthon let himself be induced to enter the political arena and to spend his days in negotiations. Against his will he had become the spokesman for the Evangelical estates. This responsibility he felt keenly; precisely for this reason he became very cautious, and sought to assure peace through negotiations. In letters to the same bishop in 1532 he expressed himself clearly over his efforts. According to his own statements, his sole concern had been to alleviate controversies. In these letters Melanchthon used a language which we scarcely find elsewhere in him. For these sharp fights, he maintained, there was no real reason at all. As he had written in his advice to the Legate Campeggio in 1524 — a memorandum that had been widely disseminated in German translation — he was ready to do his utmost to maintain the church and her practices, as long as they were to be supported from Scripture. If the extremists were excluded, peace could be maintained. To other emissaries from out-

side Germany, Melanchthon expressed himself in the
same manner. In Augsburg, when the Augsburg Confession was submitted and the *Confutation* was read, and the
schism was to be overcome in committees, Melanchthon
had taken the same position as a permanent member of
these committees. His effort was to conduct the discussions
with the greatest possible moderation and to see to it that
the opposition acted in the same way.

These statements and this procedure of Melanchthon's,
in any case, had the result that representatives of the old
faith began to think that tensions existed between Luther
and Melanchthon, and that there was an excellent chance
of separating them. Melanchthon complained strongly
about his Augsburg opponents. If it had depended on him,
he thought, the ecclesiastical tensions would have been
settled or at least mitigated. Therefore, the confessional
situation at Augsburg had not filled him with joy, as it had
Luther and others of his friends; nor had it strengthened
him in his faith. What lay on his heart was the unity of the
church which there was torn apart. Even in later years he
lamented this lost unity of the church, and was ready to try
anything to recover it.

In a letter to the same Bishop Cricius, who had taken a
great interest in him and with whom he shared humanistic
interests, Melanchthon deplores his " unhappy fate " — the
necessity of waging confessional wars instead of being able
to concentrate entirely on peaceful studies, as he wished.
Above all, he writes, he had come to realize in Augsburg
that the positive doctrines of the gospel must first be
brought into clear light before an agreement between the
two parties could be attained.

Melanchthon had not shut his eyes to union negotiations
with the Roman side. As early as 1532 he had resolved to

dedicate the revised edition of his Romans commentary to
Cardinal Albert of Mainz. A fairly long foreword should
incite the prince of the church to promote the cause of
peace. " You see how necessary peace is," wrote Melanchthon to the cardinal; " the times force us more and more
to devote ourselves to it." With the same concern he had
also turned to Erasmus and other representatives of the
old faith. Melanchthon emphasized that he was interested
in only a few basic questions. If agreement were reached on
these, the other controversies would cease by themselves.

If these views contained in the Romans commentary
achieved greater acceptance, so would the concern of the
Reformation also be understood. In the dedicatory letter
to Cardinal Albert as well as in the contemporaneous letter
to Cricius there is much rhetoric. This language dare not
be weighed too pedantically. Otherwise, one would be
forced to say, as Gustav Kawerau and others have done,
that it was a tragedy in the life of the Preceptor and also in
the cause of the Reformation, that Luther had failed to
secure a more reliable colleague. In other letters, too, one
could find dubious features. But this must be evaluated
differently; otherwise, misunderstandings and false judg-
ments are inevitable. Melanchthon was not double-
tongued. He always remained loyal to Luther and always
rejected suggestions to go over to the other camp. Of
course, his humanistic attitude misled him into pursuing
the illusion that there was a middle road upon which all
" well-intentioned and learned men " could meet. The humanists on the opposite side heard and understood this
language and were prepared to go along with him.

These thoughts, which Melanchthon had expressed in his
letters to Cardinal Albert and Bishop Cricius, appear also
in his letter to the aged Erasmus, October 25, 1532. He

speaks bitterly of the fact that both parties in the church controversy show no desire for moderation. That is why his counsels have been rejected. It seems as if the humanist Melanchthon during these years turned his attention toward his humanist friends and challenged them to concentrate all their energies on bringing peace.

The idea of " the one church " affected Melanchthon deeply. In the events of the times he saw only renewed attempts to shatter unity. Erasmus read from Melanchthon's letter that he was simply irritated by his Wittenberg colleagues. Even earlier Erasmus had expressed himself to the effect that Melanchthon had worked for the cause of peace in Augsburg and that if he, Erasmus, had had his health, he would gladly have united these efforts with his own. That Melanchthon induced him to write his last treatise, engaging in the battle of minds, *On the Lovely Peace of the Church,* is not improbable.

Melanchthon himself also testified to Erasmus in a letter that in judging dogmas he took his guidance from Erasmus, and that in judging most controversial questions he still was attached to him.

The interest of the Polish bishops in Melanchthon continued for many years. Cricius informed him that he awaited him as much as ever, and that a position would be created for him commensurate with his rank. Unfortunately, Melanchthon's answers are not extant. We do not know, therefore, how he reacted in particular. From the Italian side, however, there came similar offers. Cardinal Sadoleto wooed him. Melanchthon abstained from answering him. The common humanist basis was present here too. The French overture also belongs in this framework. The foreign humanists generally regarded Melanchthon as one of them. They thought that they held the same presuppositions and positions as he, and were thus fairly strong in their belief that they could use his influence as a moderating element in their respective lands.

Melanchthon's fame also reached France and England. Humanistic circles persuaded Francis I to invite Melanchthon to Paris. They wrote to Melanchthon that he might gladly accept this invitation in any case. He would be able to accomplish something for the freedom of the gospel and for peace in the land. The king would hear his counsel. In Germany there was doubt over the king's sincerity. Melanchthon himself hesitated, because he was not eager for discussions with the doctors of the Sorbonne, whom he had so sharply snubbed in his younger years. Thereupon, Francis I proposed private negotiations, and the Cardinal du Bellay favored this proposal. When Melanchthon now requested permission of the elector in Thorgau, the latter rejected his petition. Even when Luther personally supported this petition in Weimar, he received only a refusal. The elector, who was on his way to King Ferdinand, feared that Melanchthon's journey to Paris would damage his political negotiations. His court confirmed him in the opinion that Melanchthon would show himself too compliant away from Germany. The latter, however, was deeply offended by the elector's refusal. To his friends he complained about the elector's action. In his answer to Francis I he wrote that he had to postpone the journey until a more favorable time, but that he would continue his efforts to settle the religious controversies in a peaceful manner. The king did not abandon his attempt, and tried to attain his goal through the Smalcald League. The League, however, refused to consider his request.

More important were the negotiations that were brought to Melanchthon from England. He had already taken an interest in the church situation in England and had urged the king to support the Reformation, when he received an invitation. Luther also, who earlier had written *Against Henry, King of England,* favored this journey. The elector disapproved, but permitted a conference in Wittenberg with envoys from England. For this reason, Melanchthon composed the articles which bear the title " The Wittenberg Articles " (1536). They were brought into harmony with Luther. On this occasion a conversation on the doctrine of justification took place between Luther and Melanchthon in the presence of Bugenhagen.

The king was informed that he could be received into the Smalcald League only after he had accepted the articles. Henry VIII obviously had no interest in this stipulation. In any case, he was asked once more about his view. Until then nothing was to be undertaken by the Evangelical side on the question of the rumored church council.

The political situation was unfavorable for a *rapprochement* between the Evangelical estates in their church relations. Melanchthon pondered this fact long and seriously. Having recognized this necessity, he made contact with Martin Bucer in Strassburg. " I desire nothing more," he wrote to him, " than that the monstrous scandal of this schism, which so manifestly hinders the course of the gospel, may be eliminated." Since Luther did not oppose the new negotiations with the Upper Germans, Melanchthon requested the landgrave to promote the work of union. A great synod was not planned. The landgrave invited Melanchthon and Bucer to Kassel. During the Christmas season of 1534 they met. For Melanchthon it was not easy to advocate solely the Lutheran standpoint in the doctrine of the Lord's Supper, especially since he himself was beginning to hold a divergent view. As he later confessed, he was the representative of " an alien opinion " in Kassel. Bucer had given the assurance there that he and the Upper

German preachers agreed with Melanchthon. It was only desired to move slowly and avoid haste. A general inquiry among the leading theologians of the Lutheran persuasion yielded the consensus that Bucer and his adherents were " to be tolerated." After this decision Melanchthon took a more eager part than ever in the union efforts. Bucer meanwhile had united the Swiss theologians in a confession that differed from Melanchthon's formula so little that a final union seemed imminent. The final meeting was to take place on May 14, 1536, in Eisenach. Melanchthon was deeply apprehensive of how the affair would turn out. Since Luther was ill, the Upper Germans volunteered to come to Wittenberg. The number attending was small. Hence, no final decision was to be made, but everything was to be submitted to the estates. The decisive conversations took place in Luther's house. After Luther and Bucer had presented their viewpoints, Melanchthon was requested to draw up a union formula. This he submitted on May 29. It contained three assertions: the presence of Christ in the Sacrament, the sacramental union of Christ and the elements, and the reception of the unworthy. This declaration was subscribed to by both sides. It received the name *The Wittenberg Concord*. To be sure, it did not last long, since the Swiss would have nothing to do with Bucer's explanations, and rejected the concord. In spite of everything, however, it retained a symbolic importance.

14. The Church Council and the Religious Colloquies

The constantly reiterated demands in political circles for a church council could no longer be ignored. When the papal letter of solicitation, 1533, was brought to Saxony and Melanchthon was asked his opinion, his answer in a memorandum was that the Evangelical estates should not refuse to participate. At a council it would be possible to negotiate with the opposition under tolerable conditions. If no result were attained, one would be free of blame. By promising to take part, one assumed no obligations. Of course, he considered it necessary to point out to the emperor that it would have to be a " free council." They would not consent to be treated as defendants.

Master Philip had a foreboding that grave decisions were in the making. He saw in this affair an opportunity for the church which ought to be grasped. " Great things," he wrote, " are not without dangers." With reason, however, much may be " guided and mitigated." Furthermore, he was confident of his own cause. The basic Evangelical articles, he thought, were so clear and illuminating that no one could reject them. He placed his reliance in the Scripture and the church as " the pillar and bulwark of the truth " (I Tim. 3:15). Melanchthon saw no other means than the council to rid the world of controversies. Scripture itself pointed in this direction, he said. The elector, on the advice of his jurists, took a different position. Saxony issued a refusal. The Evangelicals saw on the papal side no guarantee of an objective treatment of the disputed questions of faith.

When the question was reopened two years later, the nuncio, Vergerio, declared that the council would be a free one. The Conference of Smalcald, in a letter drafted by Melanchthon, objected that they were not invited expressly to a " free council." By " free " he understood a meeting in which unpartisan men discussed and decided the schismatic questions according to the Word of God alone. When the nuncio in February, 1537, delivered to the Saxon elector the bull summoning the council, he received an answer that did not correspond to Melanchthon's memorandum. The latter continued firmly to assert the advantages of accepting the council. A countercouncil, such as John Frederick had considered, he rejected. He persisted in his view, however, that one could count on fairness on the part of the opposition.

Melanchthon had frequently made the proposal that before the papal nuncio came, a committee of Evangelical theologians should meet to agree on the doctrine that should be advocated at the council. Melanchthon still believed in the possibility of a settlement. Although some agreed with his plan, others thought that everything had already been said in the Augsburg Confession. Elector John Frederick resolved to deal with this question at the diet at Smalcald, 1537. At the same time he ordered Luther to draw up articles for it, "on which he proposed to stand and remain." The Smalcald Articles, as they came to be known later, underscored the Evangelicals' contrast to the Roman Church in doctrine and in practices. They were subscribed by the Wittenberg theologians Nicholas von Amsdorf, Spalatin, and Agricola before Luther submitted them on January 3, 1537, to the elector. Melanchthon added his signature with a reservation that made the elector deeply irritated at him: " I regard the above articles as right and Christian. However, concerning the pope, I hold that if he would allow the gospel, we, too, might concede to him his superiority over the bishops, which he possesses by human right, making this concession for the sake of peace and general unity among the Christians who are and may hereafter be under him."

In Smalcald a great assembly had gathered. Landgrave Philip, on Melanchthon's advice, did not submit Luther's articles for deliberation but gave the theologians the assignment to " review the Augsburg Confession, to change nothing in it, except to emphasize the papacy." Since Luther was ill, Melanchthon drew up an additional article, *On the Power and Primacy of the Pope.* The treatise, along with the Augsburg Confession and the *Apology,* was subscribed to by the theologians present. Hence, it must not be regarded as an appendix to the Smalcald Articles, which were signed there only privately on the invitation of Bugenhagen, but represented no common confession of the estates. This fact was not accurately reported to Luther and is incorrectly described by him in his preface. The new confession was not needed, since it had been determined not to attend the council. The letter of refusal had to be drafted by Melanchthon. The Evangelical powers declared that they would take part only in a free council. No one bothered about Melanchthon's opinion. He was alarmed when he saw that by this action the schism was made permanent. Full of fear over events to come, but gladdened by Luther's recovery of health, he returned to Wittenberg.

Melanchthon's views on church politics show that he was no realistic statesman, and that the actual situation did not correspond to his preconceived opinion. While still at the conference he had described his treatise as " a little sharper " than he was ordinarily accustomed to speak. At all events, he had said something clear. For the sake of the truth — so he declares in spite of his irenic attitude — even the evil consequences of separation must not deter the Evangelical estates from refusing obedience to the pope. He retained one statement that reflected the opinion of the majority: he who defends the papacy and its false doctrines makes himself guilty of error and obstructs the glory of God and the rescue of the church. This treatise contradicted the previous statements of Melanchthon, and it is unclear what motive induced him to make this complete about-face. Obviously he had wished to accommodate Luther, who was ill almost to the point of death, and he had wished to act in his place. However, other grounds also may have influenced him. In any case, Melanchthon henceforth adhered to the opinion presented therein, nor did he change it after Luther's recovery.

While Luther subsequently worked on his book *On the Councils and the Church,* Melanchthon on his own part wrote a treatise *On the Church and the Authority of the Word of God,* which undergirded his position. Luther expressed his contradiction when he said: by appeal to the fathers and councils the church will not be reformed, because they do not agree with one another.

Melanchthon, who felt called to the academic life and the education of youth, was often fated to defend his positions in public discussions. He was often indignant that the princes prevailed in these discussions. " The opinions of the unlearned are far different from the counsels of the moderate; seldom can we temper them, especially in the present tumult." Only for a short time was Melanchthon excused from public discussions. As soon as the emperor adopted a policy of moderation, Melanchthon was destined to move from one religious colloquy to another and from one imperial diet to another.

In February, 1539, Melanchthon had to accompany his elector to the Frankfurt Conference. Here Melanchthon met for the first time with the young John Calvin, who was a member of the Strassburg delegation. While the official discussions proceeded, theological conversations took place, and thereby many a misunderstanding was removed. In Frankfurt the mediators acquiesced in a fifteen-month armed truce; more they did not accomplish. However, since the council again was indefinitely postponed, there was a widespread desire in Germany to work for an ecclesiastical agreement. A religious colloquy was scheduled to meet even in the same year. Though the Curia advised against it, the emperor had to take account of the situation. On the imperial side there was real expectancy, especially since attention had been drawn to the action at Leipzig. A few months earlier a religious colloquy had taken place in Leipzig, at which two representatives from Hesse, two from Electoral Saxony, and two from Ducal Saxony had participated. The Dresden reformers attempted an ecclesiastical settlement on the basis of the first six centuries. Melanchthon and Bucer, both of whom had been participants, pointed out the impossibility of regarding the apostolic doctrine as a "rule." When Melanchthon left the colloquy at the command of his elector, it was guided to a conclusion by Bucer, and a draft of the doctrine of man and of his restoration was set forth which was destined to remain not without significance. Not only the Dresden chancellor, who had acted without the knowledge of his lord, but also some of the Evangelicals had developed the hope of further progress on this basis.

Melanchthon took part not only in the reformation in Ducal Saxony but also in that of Brandenburg. Already in 1538 he had been called to Berlin in order to submit his memorandum concerning the moderate reform of the church in Brandenburg. Here, too, the attempt was made to achieve a settlement on the basis of the humanistic spirit. Elector Joachim II, to be sure, wished to be Evangelical in doctrine, but in usages to follow the old church. He regarded it as his task to work for church union on the same basis. The " royal middle way " was to determine policy.

Melanchthon had been able to make many changes in
the elector's church order. At Joachim's behest he had to
write a report to the Catholic King Sigismund of Poland,
Joachim's father-in-law, explaining that the elector was
proceeding with the greatest moderation, allowing the gospel to be freely preached, and merely suppressing the
grossest abuses.

Although the emperor wished to undertake a religious
settlement and had already called an imperial assembly to
deal with the subject, the Evangelical estates had gathered
once more in Smalcald in March, 1540. Melanchthon composed an opinion as a suggestion of procedure. Every
schism, he wrote, had a horrible appearance. Therefore it
must be pondered whether the present schism had a com-
pelling cause. Then one could take comfort and commend
the danger to God. Melanchthon realized that, like the people of Israel in the desert, many men were becoming weary
of bearing this burden. Every Christian was placed on his
own responsibility and must accept what came, according
to God's will. For a settlement, not only doctrine but also
usages and customs must be treated. If the adversaries accepted the doctrine, some concessions could be made in externals. " But in doctrine," Melanchthon concluded, " by
God's grace we will not yield, and we pray God that he will
sustain his church and grant to princes and estates his Holy
Spirit, that they may decide and do what is right. May he
also strengthen all in suffering and danger." This time Melanchthon was more confident than other men. Melanchthon's written opinion was unanimously adopted and
confirmed with signatures. The emperor was presented a
memorial, also composed by Melanchthon, in which it was
emphasized that there would be no deviation from the
Augsburg Confession. And if Melanchthon still antici-

pated some results from a public discussion of open questions, he also realized more and more that in this area narrow bounds had been drawn.

The state of Protestantism and the situation for the negotiations at the now imminent conferences of Hagenau and Worms, of course, were greatly encumbered by a fact that also caused Melanchthon grave qualms of conscience — the bigamy of Landgrave Philip of Hesse. Exactly because the landgrave stood in such high regard among the Evangelicals, and was highly honored on account of his energy, uprightness, and loyalty, the Reformers gave him a secret confessional counsel that later brought them well-deserved reproaches and had serious consequences. On the journey to Hagenau, Melanchthon became gravely ill; it was more an emotional than a physical sickness. At Weimar, Luther encouraged him in the midst of his anxiety, and energetically resisted the desires from Hesse to defend the whole affair. Luther himself publicly retracted and admitted that he had erred.

Melanchthon did not need to travel to Hagenau. He was not excused, however, from the conference in Worms. When Melanchthon arrived there on October 31, 1540, he found a great assembly gathered. The opening dragged on. Melanchthon wrote to Camerarius: " With God's help I shall work to explain clearly, without sophistry, and with all earnestness the important doctrines for which we contend. I can do so all the more eagerly, since I have ceased to worry over the will of the princes, and thus I am more at ease than formerly." During the journey he had already worked out a memorial in which he expressed the hope that a public discussion of doctrine would be permitted and that the church would be helped thereby. He emphasized that they would clearly set forth their doctrine, in which they agreed with the universal church, and that in doing so they would appeal exclusively to Holy Scripture. They could not recognize the authority of the pope and of a council called by him; therefore, they could not accept having the papal legate as chairman of the assembly.

When the negotiations were opened by the imperial chancellor Granvella, the Cologne canonist Gropper spoke for the Catholic side, and Melanchthon for the Evangelical. He asserted that the Evangelicals deplored the schism, that they had separated from the papacy not without reason, but that they held to the foundation of the ancient church. Since private discussions were taking place, meanwhile, in which Melanchthon had no part, the colloquy between the two confessional parties did not begin until January, 1541. The Catholic side would greatly have preferred to omit this altogether and would have liked to refer the discussion of controverted questions to the committees, for the Catholic party itself was not united, whereas the Evangelical estates showed themselves more in agreement than before. Melanchthon submitted to the emperor a document in which he indicated, in the name of the Evangelicals, that they would not separate from the true church of Christ. " We contend not for power, prestige, or worldly possessions, but we cannot idly tolerate error and abuses." He warned against ambiguous forms and formulas. The straight path is always the best. Only the discussion of justification and the Mass would be difficult. Melanchthon thought, however, that even in these articles a settlement would be possible if only the truth were honored. " Since we are speaking moderately of the dignity of the bishops and administrators of the church, we are making a step toward peace; on the other hand, the bishops must permit true doctrine and the correction of abuses." Little as Melanchthon was inclined to discuss with fanatical opponents, he was not spared the necessity of crossing swords with Eck. The basis was the Augsburg Confession. True, they were able to debate only the doctrine of original sin. Eck reiterated the Roman view that the Protestants exaggerated if they called the natural weakness of men sin; Melanchthon maintained that if evil inclination is an infirmity, it still contends against the commandment of God. The discussion did not progress as far as the doctrine of justification, since the emperor abruptly adjourned the colloquy in Worms and postponed its continuation until the imperial diet in Regensburg.

The colloquy at Worms was not very encouraging to Melanchthon. His conception of agreement with the universal church could not prevail. Now other mediation proposals were made which seemed to open up greater prospects of success. With the cooperation of the landgrave, a basis for discussion was worked out in a private conference between Gropper and Bucer, on which the emperor was willing to rely. Melanchthon could expect no success from it. He thought it would lead to deceptive results. Why was it necessary to depart from the previous basis, the Augsburg Confession? Especially against the landgrave was Melanchthon now prejudiced. When Melanchthon's carriage upset on the trip to Regensburg, he took it as a bad omen for the diet. Groups had formed among the parties. Melanchthon still had the greatest confidence in Emperor Charles V. He believed that the emperor was earnestly striving for peace. Charles had great troubles, which made him wish for a united empire behind him. He wanted to form a committee that would discuss the controverted doctrines. Melanchthon opposed this and insisted that the continuation of the Worms discussion was desirable. The emperor persisted in his view, however; he selected three theologians from each side, to whom several advisers were added at the Protestants' request.

When the negotiations were opened, Chancellor Granvella presented the now-famous *Regensburg Book*. This preliminary document had been worked out in Worms in the private conference between Gropper and Bucer, and was meant to form the basis for the settlement. Elector Joachim II had previously shown it to John Frederick and Luther, and expressed the opinion that the emperor would probably accept it. Joachim was informed of the origin of this writing; he knew that in the main it had been composed by scholars of the other side. If agreement were reached on original sin, justification, and the Sacraments, then all the other deviations would be settled automatically. Luther had already said to Elector Joachim at the time: " These people mean well, but those are impossible proposals. Resorting to such means is vain." Nevertheless, at the emperor's wish it was accepted as the basis for the colloquy, without disclosing its authorship. Melanchthon found the book completely ambiguous. It would be more useful, he said, to call things by their right names, and to say, " A ship is a ship." When he went through the book with the landgrave, the latter had already examined it and marked the offensive passages. The landgrave was firmer than had been expected. The mistrust toward Melanchthon also was shown to be unjustified, and Luther encouraged him to persevere.

Melanchthon was again the chief spokesman against Eck. Before every session a conference was held by the Evangelical theologians. Calvin had come again with the Strassburgers and participated. The first four articles, on man before and after the Fall, were accepted without alteration.

Over the article on justification, which in this draft contained "many alien opinions," the strongest opposition arose. The Evangelicals saw no possibility of progress by means of the article of the *Book,* so they bypassed it and tried to achieve an advance in free discussion. Melanchthon showed no desire to continue, but the other Evangelical representatives pressed him not to break off the discussion. After many efforts by Eck, Melanchthon, and Cardinal Contarini, with the energetic cooperation of Gropper, a union formula was found which after several changes was accepted.

The unexpected had happened: union on the subject of justification was achieved. This took place May 2, 1541. Melanchthon saw the chief points of the Evangelical faith proclaimed in it, though he also missed certain things there. Luther and his elector expressed themselves not as favorably as Calvin, who wrote to Farel: " You will marvel when you see what has been obtained from the adversaries. Our side has upheld the summary of the true doctrine. There is nothing in the formula which is not found in our writings." To the Saxon elector the formula seemed too opaque and sprawling. And when Luther found nothing good in the amended formula, he nevertheless asked the princes not to treat Melanchthon too harshly, lest he die of grief. The representatives of the Catholic side considered the amended article in need of supplementation. The Legate Contarini may have given it his approval, and in his report to Rome he may have expressed joy over the attainment of the goal, but Rome was of another opinion. Despite Contarini's explanatory treatise *On Justification,* the Consistory repudiated the article on justification, and thereby nullified the already announced union in doctrine.

How little agreement had actually been attained was re-

vealed by the fact that in the articles concerning the
church and the Sacraments a violent battle broke out. Melanchthon wanted to withdraw from the colloquy. He had
hoped to do away with the *Regensburg Book*. He openly
declared that he could not and would not approve of the
language of the book. In other respects, too, he showed
himself so unyielding that the emperor summoned Landgrave Philip and asked him to use his influence on Melanchthon. The net result of the colloquy, however, was
that now there were three parties. The majority wished
to hear no more of an " accommodation of religion." Even
the project of tolerance had no prospect of success; the emperor had to regard his union policy as a failure.

On order of the Evangelical authorities, Melanchthon
drew up a report of the religious colloquy and declared in
retrospect that it had been necessary to oppose the *Regensburg Book*. " The lords may do what they think best; as
for me and others like me, however, we are obligated to
teach Christian doctrine rightly and purely and to pray
God to sustain and protect his church, and so I do not
doubt that he will not let this light be wholly suppressed."
Melanchthon also wrote the final declarations of the Evangelical estates. In them it was said that they accepted the
harmonized doctrinal statements in the sense of the Augsburg Confession and the *Apology*. After a five-month absence Melanchthon returned to Wittenberg.

Corresponding to the emperor's desire, the pope now
wished to open a council in Trent. The papal bull was
read at the imperial diet at Nuremberg in 1542. Melanchthon did not believe that the council would take place so
long as war still raged between the emperor and Francis I.
In this judgment he was correct. But political events in
Germany also held out no good prospects. The overthrow

of the Duke of Cleves cast dark shadows ahead. When Melanchthon received orders to prepare himself to attend the 1544 imperial diet at Speyer, he only wished that the Evangelical princes were united and might remember that " now the moment of decision has come, on which life and death depend! " Seeing no advance preparations on the Evangelical side, he declared: " If important matters are treated at the diet, I shall only follow the Lord." Melanchthon saw another era emerging. The mood at diets and conferences was becoming sharper, and war was foreseen. He did not need to travel to Speyer, for the ecclesiastical negotiations were postponed. Thoughts of the coming religious colloquy already caused him anxiety, and even pursued him into his dreams. He no longer aimed at seeking new formulations of the Evangelical doctrine. He wished to fall back to the position that it had already been clearly enough stated elsewhere. Only on externals, on the power of the bishops, and on the spiritual courts did he wish to say anything.

For the Diet of Worms in 1545 Melanchthon was destined for the last time to draft a memorial. In the name of the Wittenberg theologians he set forth the so-called " Wittenberg Reformation." " A true Christian church government," he wrote there, " consists principally of these five parts: pure doctrine, right use of the Sacraments, maintenance of the office of preaching, right discipline, and schools." The elector was not satisfied with it. It was his opinion that " Master Philip has not put enough work into it and has not stated it in a sufficiently distinguished manner "; however, he gave it his aproval. It was sent to the landgrave and to the elector Palatine: the latter incorporated it into the foundation of his order for the reformation of the church. John Frederick also had Melanchthon

compose a petition to the emperor, saying that the Protestants did not oppose union in matters of faith, but that
they had to reject the council called at Trent.

The situation in the empire had changed considerably.
The emperor demanded that the Protestants submit to the
council. These, however, demanded a prolongation of
peace. To gain time, he then postponed the colloquy to the
following diet at Regensburg. What was this colloquy to
do, however, when the council opened in Trent on December 13, 1545? The colloquy was opened, nevertheless, in
the hope of inducing the Protestants to yield and to attend the council. Melanchthon was happy that he was not
required to be present. The participants at their own wish
received an opinion composed by Melanchthon, which
once more set forth clearly the position of the Wittenbergers.

During the discussions in Regensburg, Luther died. His
death set loose a wave of deep mourning on the Evangelical
side. Melanchthon had found him milder during the last
months, and had been able to converse with him entirely
without embarrassment. He related to his friends that in
December, 1545, they had had a searching discussion on
the question of the Lord's Supper. The report has been
widely doubted, but it appears thoroughly credible. Luther
is said to have remarked: " I must confess that we have
gone much too far on the subject of the Supper." He was
unwilling to publish a statement modifying the previous
conception, said Melanchthon, lest he bring the entire doctrine into suspicion. The matter should be commended to
God.

When Luther rode with Jonas on January 23, 1546, to
his birthplace, Eisleben, in order to reconcile the quarreling counts of Mansfeld with one another, Melanchthon re-

mained behind in Wittenberg. They did not see each other again. In his letters to Luther the Preceptor once again gives expression to his respect and gratitude. He calls Luther the restorer of true doctrine and his dearest father. Luther did not receive his last letter; he had died February 18. This news was a heavy blow to Melanchthon. Now he stood completely alone. The whole church was robbed of the leader and teacher whom God had raised up. With deep emotion he broke the news to the students in his lecture: " Gone is Dr. Martin Luther, who in these last times of the world was the leader of the church." When the funeral procession from Eisleben reached Wittenberg on February 22, Bugenhagen preached the sermon in the Castle Church, while Melanchthon delivered the Latin memorial address. Without hesitation he placed Luther beside Paul and Augustine, and extolled him as the hero of faith, who had courageously withstood every danger. A significant link in the chain of the teachers of the church, he had set the Word on a lampstand, purified divine worship, built the church " with trowel and sword." In his warfare he had kept the faith and maintained a good conscience. His achievement, therefore, would remain unforgotten through all time, and his piety would have an exemplary influence. Melanchthon's anxiety was directed toward the forsaken children who had lost a wonderful father. With trembling voice he delivered this address, which ended in a prayer of gratitude.

When the elector on this occasion turned to the university and summoned it to guard Luther's heritage faithfully, Melanchthon as usual had to draft the answer. This he did in strong words which reflected his own conviction.

15. The War, the Interim, and the Religious Peace

The Diet of Regensburg, 1546, revealed the plans of the emperor. In order to bring peace to the empire, Charles V wished to force Elector John Frederick and Landgrave Philip of Hesse into submission, as " disobedient, disloyal, and obstinate destroyers of the common peace." Then the Protestants were to bow to the church council. To the neighboring states he directed the summons to fight the heretics in common cause with him. Melanchthon, who had continued to place hope in the emperor, finally had his eyes opened. He thought that he could already recognize the victory of the emperor in the position of the stars. At the same time, however, he saw that this victory would be accompanied by grave consequences. Therefore, he admonished his friends to bear misfortune courageously, and as early as July, 1546, he composed a tract, *Reasons Why the Churches of the Augsburg Confession Cling Firmly to Their Doctrine, and Cannot Recognize the Judges Assembled at Trent.* In this writing he wished to make clear the motives out of which the Reformation arose, in order then to vindicate the action of the Protestants in the present. " We have no pleasure in schism, and we recognize our danger clearly, but we cannot allow the light of the gospel again to be extinguished and the doctrine salutary to the church to be suppressed." To strengthen the people, he also republished Luther's tract of 1530, *Warning to His Dear Germans,* with a timely preface. His aim was to tell the individual what his duty was in this crisis. He should not be misled into inaction by false notions. Resistance is self-defense, he said, and as such is just as clearly commanded in a case of the suppression of the true faith as

when a murderer invades a house. Things had had to go
far before Melanchthon, the man of compliance and of
peace, issued such a summons.

When the war broke out and the Evangelical allies, despite several successes, allowed much time to slip away, Melanchthon became deeply troubled. He was truly dismayed
when Duke Maurice of Saxony showed himself prepared
to form an alliance with the emperor and to execute the
imperial ban upon his cousin. In November, 1546, Wittenberg was occupied by Spanish troops. Melanchthon remained in the town until the last moment, then he moved
with his family and Luther's widow to Zerbst. Friends
helped him so that he would not be in want. At first he did
not know where to turn. Should he remain in Saxony or
go to Tübingen, where the duke had earlier offered him a
place to work? To all his misery and distress was added do-
mestic sorrow. His daughter Anna, the wife of Sabinus,
died in Königsberg. In this state of affairs Melanchthon
composed a little tract of consolation, *Loci consolationis.*
The Christian must bow under the hand of God. Misfortune never happens by chance, but is God's will. If man is
visited by misfortune, God does not mean to destroy him
but to call him to repentance and to faith. Therefore, faith
takes refuge in God and says with Job: " Though he slay
me, yet will I trust in him." Melanchthon also drew comfort from the thought that the church of God will always
abide.

A few months later the outcome had been reached. Elector John Frederick had been defeated by the emperor on
the Lochau Heath and captured. According to the provi-
sions of the Wittenberg Capitulation he remained the pris-
oner of the emperor, lost his electoral dignity to Duke
Maurice, and likewise his lands with the exception of cer-

tain Thuringian districts. When the emperor had entered
Wittenberg, Melanchthon felt unsafe in Zerbst and went
farther on to Brunswick and then to Nordhausen. He still
hoped that he would be able to return to Wittenberg. The
new elector wished to restore the university. At the territorial diet which he held in Leipzig, he also called Melanchthon and the other Wittenberg professors and declared to them that he would change nothing in the state
of religion. Although the rebuilding of the university cost
Melanchthon much concern, he declined calls to go elsewhere. The imprisoned old elector advised his sons to
transfer from the University of Wittenberg to Jena. They
also called Melanchthon thither. The latter protracted the
negotiations, because he did not want to give up Wittenberg, the nursery of the Reformation. In Weimar, men
spoke of ingratitude and disloyalty, and reproached him
that he had placed himself on the side of the hated " Judas
of Meissen." Melanchthon, however, felt himself obligated
to offer further service to the church of Saxony. The
change of rule changed nothing in that regard. He begged
people to understand his decision to remain in Wittenberg.

While he resumed his old position there, the Saxon
dukes attached themselves to the strict Lutheran party in
contradiction to him. The school in Jena was manned with
extreme pupils of Luther's. Meanwhile, the emperor, who
had not agreed with the conciliar policy of the pope, proposed personally to undertake the reorganization of ecclesiastical relations in Germany. Disregarding the council,
which had been transferred from Trent to Bologna, he
held a diet at Augsburg in September, 1547, which was to
deal primarily with the question of religion.

When Elector Maurice in these circumstances demanded

from the Wittenbergers a memorandum on the establishment of religious peace, Melanchthon admonished him to do nothing in haste and not to accept the Tridentine decrees, which contained so much that was untrue. While the committee of the estates was unclear how to proceed, the emperor secretly had a book prepared, on which, along with Bishops Pflug and Helding, John Agricola collaborated. In it the doctrine of justification was set forth in a Catholicizing fashion, the Mass was interpreted as a commemorative sacrifice, and the Lord's Supper under both forms and the marriage of the clergy were referred to the council for decision. In questions of papal power, the doctrine of transubstantiation, and church practices the Protestants received no concessions. When the emperor delivered this book to the estates, at all events, he learned to his surprise that Elector Maurice himself resisted him. Charles V complained that Melanchthon had already encouraged John Frederick in his disobedience to the emperor, and now was actively disturbing the negotiations. With this animosity prevailing against him, Melanchthon did not need to come to Augsburg. Pressed on all sides, in spite of his gentleness, he was now the most hated of men. It seemed that the emperor would disregard every resistance and would dictate terms in questions of faith.

Melanchthon thoroughly examined the *Augsburg Interim,* which in his judgment betrayed a certain affinity for the *Regensburg Book.* Little as he wished to burden his conscience, he still was required by the elector to examine the book. He wrote a first opinion on the basic principles of the book and a further one dealing with justification and the Mass, showing that here justification was ascribed to man's own merit and was traced back to love instead of to faith.

Just as little could he accept the sacrificial character of the Mass. Before they traveled to Augsburg, he discussed his objections with other theologians. " The Augsburg formula is a piece of patchwork," he wrote; " it mixes good and bad together and plays with sophistry." That was a clear word. Elector Maurice could gather from it that the men in Saxony had no liking for the *Interim*. In Melanchthon's private letters, however, we read how the *Interim* weighed upon him. It was clear to him that the truth was falsified in it, superstition promoted, and finally new dissension conjured up. The elector was not satisfied with the opinion, since it did not fit his policy. For this reason, he had his adviser Christopher von Carlowitz exert his influence on Melanchthon in order to win him for the *Interim*. What Carlowitz wrote to him and how he threatened him, we do not know. Only Melanchthon's reply is extant, which he must have written to the Saxon statesman in deepest depression. Melanchthon insisted that he was not rebellious and that he was willing to endure everything which the elector prescribed. Under Luther he had endured a kind of dependence which had been hard for him, he said. He had not provoked the controversy, but had been drawn into it, and by his moderation he had evoked dissatisfaction and hatred from those who now described themselves as peacemakers — he was referring to Agricola. He had conceded much, in order vehemently to contest other points. He was prepared to recognize the episcopal order and the papal prestige as formulated in the *Interim*. He would even accept the ancient practices. But in doctrinal questions his objections were justified; the truth must be preferred to life itself.

When Carlowitz made use of this letter, Melanchthon's enemies triumphed and called him a turncoat. In his own

circle Melanchthon was attacked and reproached most violently; in connection with it he experienced considerable
grief. He was no diplomat, and he did not understand how
to guide the common cause. He trusted all men, and was
amazed when others abused his trust. Thus Melanchthon's
letter to Carlowitz is only to be understood from the threats
with which the latter managed to win him for his pur-
poses.

While the *Augsburg Interim* was being further sharpened in the sense of the decrees of Trent, the Wittenbergers indeed did not fail to oppose it by means of further
opinions composed by Melanchthon. They pointed out
that the understanding of faith was inadequate, pure doctrine was obscured, and much was taught that was false.
The preponderance of the Catholic party, however, was so
great that the *Interim* was proclaimed unchanged and was
elevated into imperial law. In its 26 chapters the Protestants were ordered to accept the Roman conception of
church and tradition, of merit and works, of the seven sacraments and the invocation of saints. Married priests were
permitted to retain their marriages pending the council's
decision. What the Reformation had achieved seemed to
have been demolished at a blow.

Although the *Interim* was put into effect in South Germany by means of force, it could not be carried out in
North Germany. When Maurice of Saxony tried to introduce it in his land, he first summoned Melanchthon to
Leipzig and requested a memorandum from him. It was
disseminated in print, and was the first public protest
against the coercive imperial mandate. If the church in
Saxony accepted the *Interim,* concluded Melanchthon, it
would manifest that it had formerly taught falsely. That
would bring many men into grave temptation; moreover,

it would be blasphemy. "Though war and destruction
now threaten, we must regard God's commandment more
highly, namely, we must not deny the known truth of the
gospel." God's commandment demands an act of confession. Or should men reintroduce false doctrine and idol-
atry? Should they destroy what had been built up in their
land through God's grace? Should the pure worship of God
be annulled? The Wittenberg theologians stood behind
Melanchthon and declared that they neither would nor
could change the true doctrine. No creature has power to
change divine truth. Moreover, no man must be led into
denying the known truth.

Elector Maurice was in a difficult position. Obligated to
the emperor on the one side, on the other hand, hard
pressed by the attitude of his people, he did not yet dare to
resist the emperor openly. He endeavored to find a middle
way at the territorial diet at Meissen. Melanchthon's mind
was eased when he saw that the Saxon estates wished to
strike everything false out of the *Interim*. The work was
completed in a few days and gathered together by Melanchthon. Although this action against the *Interim* was
still not sharp enough to satisfy many, the elector rejected
it. He wanted the estates to resolve upon further compliance. Again the situation looked dark to Melanchthon, and
he thought that the same fate would befall them as had
overtaken the Swabians who had not accepted "the imperial sphinx." Conversations at the territorial diet in Torgau, meanwhile, produced no further results. Melanchthon, it is true, urged that they should yield and suffer,
rather than appear defiant. When his memorandum appeared in print, not at his initiative, however, the imperial
party once again flew into a rage and demanded his ban-
ishment from Saxony. At that time, like Martin Bucer, he

could have gone to England, whither Archbishop Cranmer had invited him. Elector Maurice was now satisfied with his declaration, however, and took him under his protection.

Negotiations over the *Interim* were not yet at an end in Saxony. In November, 1548, new discussions had to be held in Leipzig. Especially the theologians were aroused that not only Marian festivals but even the Corpus Christi festival were to be celebrated. With inward resistance they consented to these resolutions. They knew that they had " considerably burdened " themselves with the *Leipzig Interim* (the version of the *Interim* imposed upon Maurice's domains) , and begged that these resolutions be carried into practice only gradually. Although they accepted them " out of obedience to His Imperial Majesty and love for peace," they were unwilling under any circumstances to acknowledge the bishops' jurisdiction. The negotiations over the *Interim* had shown what serious consequences the territorial church government could have. The concessions that Melanchthon had announced himself prepared to accept concerned only externals, it is true, but even these could have grave consequences. Later, Melanchthon admitted that he had refrained from further resistance in order to avoid rebellion. Nothing would have been accomplished by his resistance. The good intention of saving what still could be saved excused him, he thought. In later writings, however, he stated clearly that the elector had gone too far with the *Interim* and had interfered with things which were not his business. Thanks to Melanchthon, no changes in doctrine had been introduced in Wittenberg through the *Interim*. The elector himself took no offense that the white clerical gown was not used in Wittenberg's public worship. Melanchthon had foreseen that the changes prescribed by the law would soon disappear again.

Pope Julius III had reopened the council in Trent on May 1, 1551; shortly before, the emperor had demanded that the Protestants send delegates to it. In Dresden it was discussed what attitude should be taken. Melanchthon thought that it would be better to attend the council; it must only be assured in advance that they should not fall into a false position. They were agreed that they would stand on the doctrine of the Augsburg Confession and the Catechism. At bottom, Melanchthon expected nothing from the council. He wished in vain, however, that the elector would send someone else instead of him. To him fell the task of writing an explanation of the Augsburg Confession for the council, which the envoys were to submit there, not in the name of the princes, to be sure, but only of the theologians.

Melanchthon went with Camerarius to Dessau, in order to work on this writing undisturbed. Thus in 1551 appeared *The Repetition of the Augsburg Confession,* which later in printed form was named *The Saxon Confession.* Starting from the present situation, Melanchthon described in it the course of the Reformation and its progress, in order then to enumerate the Roman abuses with all possible clarity. As had been his opinion for a long time, he emphasized that the church of the Reformation agreed in doctrine with the ancient church. After discussing the foundations of Evangelical doctrine, he summarized all dogmas in the two sentences: " I believe in the forgiveness of sins " and " I believe in the holy Christian church." To every Roman error he set the Evangelical view in contrast, so that it would immediately be clear by comparison which side deserved preference. It was no confession of Evangelical doctrine alone, but was at the same time a refutation

of the Roman Church, its theology and its cultus. Melanchthon intended to say nothing new, nor to raise any
new discussion, but to affirm what the Reformation had
taught from the beginning. Simultaneously this renewed
confession brought to expression the fact that the *Interim*
was now dead. In order to give the " Repetition " confessional status, it was first subscribed by all the professors
and superintendents of the Saxon church, then by the theologians of Pomerania and numerous others, who thereby
ratified the work of Melanchthon. The assent that he received was a great satisfaction to Melanchthon, especially
since the Württemberg Confession composed by Brentz for
the same purpose coincided in content with his writing.

When the first session of the council was announced for
January, 1552, Melanchthon received the order to prepare
for the journey. In Nuremberg he was to await further instructions. The electoral councillors were already in Trent,
where they had been granted a hearing in a " congrega-
tion." A letter of safe conduct was drawn up for Melanchthon. Meanwhile, the clangor of arms grew louder and
louder, so that it would have been folly to go on to Trent.
Melanchthon remained in Nuremberg, worked busily
there on theological tasks, and then returned to Wittenberg, when the sudden advance of Elector Maurice upon
Innsbruck broke up the council. The result of this mili-
tary campaign, however, was a complete change of the situation.

The Treaty of Passau promised an imperial diet to confer on the question of religion. Before this took place, the
Evangelical princes gathered their theologians in Naumburg to clarify preliminary questions. The number of participants was small; consequently, the basis for discussion
drafted by Melanchthon was not discussed in detail. They

decided that they would refuse unconditionally to accept papal doctrine or the *Interim,* and would appeal only to the Augsburg Confession. " One harmonious body cannot be made out of the persecutors and our churches; thus it has been found with the *Interim* that this patchwork is impossible." In February, 1555, the Diet of Augsburg was then opened by King Ferdinand. After negotiations lasting for months, the diet granted the territorial lords free choice in religion. No longer was there talk of requiring them to follow the emperor or the pope in matters of religion. Melanchthon had not participated in these transactions, nor had he assessed the great importance of the Religious Peace.

VII

The Last Battles

16. DISSENSION IN HIS OWN CAMP

Much as Melanchthon had exerted himself in behalf of all Protestantism during the critical years after the Smalcald War, the great work that he had taken upon himself with the Saxon Confession and with numerous memoranda had not been generally accepted. The Wittenberg Preceptor now stood under the reproach of being compliant and of having failed to resist the *Interim* sufficiently. In Wittenberg many years earlier, in 1533, he had seen to it that preachers and candidates for teaching positions in the church should be bound by an oath. On the basis of the form used in Wittenberg he now drew up a set of articles for Mecklenburg for the examination of preachers before ordination. This examination was then widely adopted by other churches, and enjoyed high esteem. The fight over questions of theology and church in the Protestant camp made his life difficult, however, and he longed for a release from theological controversies. Especially must it have hurt him that some of his own former pupils, filled with fanatical dogmatism, turned against him and tried to discredit him everywhere. The Preceptor was not altogether without fault. He had given many of them occasion to quarrel with him. Not only had the negotiations over nonessentials made him appear weak; he had not sufficiently resisted the introduction of unnecessary and harmful practices, and he himself had admitted that he had not handled the affair of the *Interim* correctly. For him the pure proclamation of the gospel was all-important, and he emphasized as its most important points the doctrine of justification and the understanding of the church; however, in this case he had not taken sufficient care for their protection.

Melanchthon felt weary and old, especially when the burden of responsibility for the entire church rested upon him. He was no longer able to assess the situation correctly, and he lacked the toughness and endurance to defend his own position. He was of a different character from Bucer, who allowed himself to be banished from Strassburg by the *Interim,* or Brentz, who in the same year left Schwä-bisch-Hall for a life of destitution. Brentz, and later Calvin also, objected earnestly that the *Interim* could not be taken so lightly, but that even in church practices must be seen an instance of the obligatory confession of the faith *(casus confessionis)*. More vehemently and passionately and insistently than all the others, however, proceeded his former pupil, Matthew Vlacich (Flacius), of Illyria. When the negotiations over the *Interim* began in Saxony, he shook the dust of Wittenberg from his feet and went to Magdeburg, from which he carried on a lengthy, unpleasant feud with Melanchthon, which added greatly to the confusion of the situation.

From Magdeburg, Flacius circulated numerous pamphlets. In one year there were over ninety writings. Magdeburg soon was dubbed " the chancellery of God and Christ " by his adherents. The writings of Flacius betokened bitter things for Melanchthon. At first he wished to ignore them, but later he saw that he would have to answer the "Slavic fugitive." Moderate as his answer was, it aroused Flacius to ever more violent attacks. He accused Melanchthon of falsifying the truth, because he deviated not only in questions of church practice but also in those of faith. Nonessentials, he held, were things which were placed at the individual's free option, but if they were elevated into law they ceased to have the status of nonessentials. Flacius reproached the Wittenberg theologians that they had sacrificed the glory of God to their fear of men.

Under Flacius' stimulation the Hamburg preachers also turned to Melanchthon on the same question of " indifferent things." The superintendent John Aepinus asked whether it was right " to tolerate a certain servitude in nonessentials and not leave the church, if the civil authorities imposed this servitude upon it." Imploringly he added: " Toward you the eyes of many are directed; on your judgment hangs a great part of Christendom. You dare not allow those who place so great trust in you to remain in doubt and uncertainty." Melanchthon was touched by this letter. He emphasized in his answer that they had altered neither doctrine nor public worship in Wittenberg. " Since we have greater matters to defend, let us abandon the dissension over nonessentials." Like an entreaty sounds the further sentence: " It behooves men of good will not to be too hasty in condemning us." He at least was unwilling that the example of Swabia should be repeated in Saxony.

But he was not finished with controversy. Further violent battles still faced Melanchthon. Although at first he wanted to regard them merely as differences in expression, actual points of dispute were involved.

Andrew Osiander, one of the most influential Nuremberg preachers, advocated views reminiscent of German mysticism. In 1530 at Augsburg he had complained to Melanchthon that his views were not adopted into the Augsburg Confession. Now, when he was called to Königsberg as first professor in the university after having been exiled from his homeland by the *Interim*, a severe dissension broke out in which theologians from all over Germany took part. At Königsberg, Osiander again advocated his peculiar teachings of the substantial righteousness of Christ and its indwelling in man. Justification he understood in the sense of a " being made righteous " rather than a " being declared righteous." In his speculations over Christ he went so far that the human nature in Christ was overlooked, and the work that he accomplished as man lost its significance. For him as for every mystic, the historical act of the Savior receded into the background, and contact with his divine nature alone bestowed righteousness.

Melanchthon was directly hit when Andrew Osiander turned against him in the doctrine of justification. As Melanchthon confessed to his friend Camerarius, this controversy stirred men's hearts far more than the one over ministerial gowns. That the controversy assumed such proportions was due not alone to Osiander, but at the same time to the violent manner in which the pupils of Melanchthon reacted to this doctrine. The genuinely Lutheran motifs in Osiander were misjudged and his partially mystical views were not understood. Osiander was so deeply convinced of his agreement with Luther, to which John Brentz also referred later, that he expressed himself in sharpest fashion over the opposing views of Melanchthon and his pupils. Melanchthon had recognized that substantial differences existed between them, and therefore he proposed a personal discussion. Since this never took place and the controversy dragged on, Melanchthon wrote his *Reply to the Book of the Rev. Andrew Osiander,* in which he ex-

pounded his position once again: The ground of our redemption, he thinks, is the whole Christ, and in faith in
him man receives forgiveness, and this not merely because
of his regeneration. Faith in forgiveness must first be present; only then can Christ dwell in us and do his work in us.
The record of the conversation between Luther and Melanchthon in 1536 over justification was not accepted by
Osiander. This battle cut Melanchthon to the heart, since
Osiander issued one polemical tract after another, and asserted that either Melanchthon's pupils did not understand him or else Melanchthon himself had forsaken Luther's doctrine. According to him, Melanchthon did not
understand the meaning of justification.

Duke Albert of Prussia, who wished to settle the controversy and had proposed a discussion in Frankfurt, could
accomplish nothing; he sent Osiander's writings to all
Evangelical authorities, complained against Melanchthon,
and called for a decision. Obviously Melanchthon had not
grasped the view of Osiander clearly enough; its mystical
character was beyond his comprehension, and thus he
treated it as approximating Roman Catholic doctrine. The
Swabian John Brentz had a better understanding, and protested against Melanchthon's criticism. While Melanchthon emphasized the cross as the foundation of acquired
righteousness, Osiander taught the indwelling of Christ,
the substantial righteousness of Christ, and rejected the
imputed righteousness as a fiction. Here there was too
much unclarity, which Melanchthon had to reject. Even
God's indwelling, of which Osiander spoke so much, in his
opinion obscured the work and merit of Christ. This indwelling of God, which for Osiander was the cause of justification, can at most be designated the result of justification according to Melanchthon. Melanchthon's written

opinion, which turned out to be basically moderate, particularly enraged Osiander, who again launched coarse invectives against him.

Duke Albert wished to use Brentz to clarify the situation, since the latter stood closest to Osiander. Nevertheless, Brentz's attempts at arbitration brought little satisfaction. At this point in the controversy Osiander died. The princes wished that the whole affair might be brought to an end at a conference. No longer was there a Luther who could settle such tensions with inherent authority. Duke Albert saw in Osiander a good and honorable man, and even tried to vindicate his honor after his death. Melanchthon should plead the cause. The question had a certain importance, since Osiander had adherents not only in Prussia but also in Pomerania and in Nuremberg. Melanchthon and Runge, of Greifswald, even had to make a journey to Nuremberg. The result was that Osiander's teachings were banned from the church. Even though they contained an element of that which gave Luther's teaching its depth, they were impossible because of their exaggerations and their rigor. Melanchthon here was acting not on his own behalf, he was representing the cause of Protestantism. By order of the princes, at the Naumburg Conference of 1554, he wrote a decision in which he made it clear that much in Osiander was obscure, but also that much was incorrect. Had Osiander lived longer, he himself would surely have amended the offensive passages. The fight with Osiander's followers continued in Prussia, however, so that Duke Albert had to request Melanchthon and Brentz again in 1556 to provide for peace in the Prussian church. Finally the Osiandrians capitulated and accepted the Wittenberg doctrine. Gradually, Melanchthon had become milder in his judgment of this tendency, too, and conceded that too much had at first been deduced from Osiander's statements in reference to the doctrine of Christ's mediatorial office and to justification.

Fanaticism such as Flacius had kindled in his fight against Melanchthon meanwhile came more and more violently to the fore. Under these circumstances the Preceptor had to defend himself against increasing attacks. New accusations were raised against his teaching. His doctrine of justification was declared incorrect; he was alleged to have falsified the central doctrine of Protestantism.

For some time Melanchthon had attached great importance to the activity of faith, and had occasionally used the expression that one could speak of faith only when it produces good works. Back in the 1530's he had met objections in this connection. However, when his pupil George Major sharpened this thesis still further and asserted that no one could be saved without true repentance, the storm of contradiction broke not only over Major in Mansfeld but also over his teacher, Melanchthon. Flacius and Amsdorf raised the charge that through this view of justification Melanchthon wished to promote the acceptance of the Roman doctrine. Thereby they obscured the position of the Wittenbergers and made them appear to advocate the idea that works are the cause of salvation. All of northern Germany arose against Major, who was deprived of his superintendency and went to Wittenberg. In the meantime the Flacians turned their weapons against Melanchthon himself. They incessantly leveled against him the accusations that he weakened the Lutheran conception, mixed predestination into justification, defended " Stoic necessity," and so on, until Melanchthon finally dismissed their attack with sharp words.

Flacius, it is true, proposed a reconciliation to Melanchthon, suggesting a meeting between them in Coswig, a city lying between Wittenberg and Magdeburg. What he had in mind, however, was not candidly stated. He wished to humiliate the Preceptor, to summon him before his bar of judgment in order to abjure false doctrines. When Melanchthon heard about the articles that he was to confess before Flacius, he refused to appear at this colloquy. Flacius thereupon demanded of him a public recantation.

Wittenberg University was irritated by the Flacians. Satirical poems appeared, among which was one on " The Synod of the Birds," who after the death of the swan wished to elect a new king. Some favored the nightingale (*philomela*), others the cuckoo, the blackbird, or the cock. As the greatest screecher the cuckoo was almost made king, and he now persecuted the nightingale and his followers. Flacius in Coswig complained about these Wittenberg satires. Peace did not ensue. Melanchthon declared that he always submitted to the judgment of the church, but not to that of an individual. The affair no longer concerned a single point of doctrine, but the whole. Envoys who came to him from Coswig believed that a consensus in doctrine should be established. In extreme agitation, however, Melanchthon rejected the one-sided proposal that they brought. Nevertheless, for the sake of peace, he expressed his mind over the articles submitted to him. Since the age leaned toward sophistry, he preferred to say what he meant, instead of allowing false interpretations to arise. From the other side also efforts were undertaken to frustrate the rupture in the church. Melanchthon took these attacks very much to heart. He saw that a gulf separated him from Flacius, who now became professor in Jena. While they were fighting each other, they were failing to preserve their advantage afforded by the Religious Peace of Augsburg.

17. CONFERENCE AND SYNOD

After the Religious Peace of Augsburg, 1555, still another conference of theologians was to be held, in order to take up the legal questions again and to strengthen peace in the empire. Another imperial diet came to nothing, and on August 24, 1557, the meeting of theologians was convened at Worms. It was to be the last attempt to reconcile Roman Catholics and Protestants. No one, least of all Melanchthon, had much hope of success. However, out of regard for the soon-to-be-elected emperor, the estates permitted the religious colloquy. It was the disunity of the Protestants that caused the greatest difficulties. The Evangelical princes in June summoned a meeting of princes in Frankfurt, in which several theologians also participated. Here a memorial in a Melanchthonian sense was drawn up. Even the Swiss looked forward to Worms. Calvin wished that Melanchthon could arrange a special colloquy with him there. Meanwhile, Elector August of Saxony detained Melanchthon, since his brother-in-law, the King of Denmark, had asked him to bring Melanchthon along on his visit. Again Melanchthon was reminded of Hassfurt's horoscope. After some delay, however, the elector sent him to Worms, where his presence was more important than at a little Danish synod. The leading theologians of both sides had gathered there. From the background Flacius inflamed his adherents. When Melancthon arrived, the majority sided with him. The Jena men accomplished nothing.

This quarrel was eagerly watched on the Roman Catholic side. The Jena men did not wish to take part until the Zwinglians, Osiander, Major, and the Adiaphorists were condemned. Melanchthon then delivered a great speech, since he saw the attack directed at himself. He gave a declaration of his views, and emphasized that he considered it childish to continue quarreling over these points. After sharp words were exchanged, the men parted. The Flacians were dubbed disturbers of the peace. The colloquy was dissolved on the ground that the Protestants were divided. With a heavy heart, Melanchthon had already traveled to Worms. The behavior of the Flacians greatly troubled him. Above all, their demand to issue condemnations wounded him deeply.

Melanchthon was affected no less by these contentions than by the Lord's Supper controversy which had broken out afresh. This was carried out between Hamburg and Geneva. Joachim Westphal leveled a violent attack at Calvin, who on his part urgently challenged Melanchthon to enter this quarrel. If the Master remained silent, so he thought, he would only give a greater incentive to his opponents. Calvin pressed Melanchthon to declare himself publicly upon the doctrine of the Lord's Supper and to dispel all misunderstandings. Obviously Calvin had not noticed that Melanchthon, despite his friendly attitude toward him, did not share his theology. Least of all, however, did Melanchthon approve of hateful contentions. Now the Flacians wanted to brand him a Crypto-Calvinist. The quarrel played itself out in Bremen, where the Dutch preachers Tieman and Hardenberg squared off until Hardenberg had to quit the field.

Count Palatine Otto Henry would gladly have gained Melanchthon for Heidelberg. The opportunity to escape the controversy in Saxony was tempting to him. And yet he now declined the call, just as he had declined a little earlier to transfer to Strassburg. He renounced the chance to return to his native land.

True, he left Worms to follow a deferential invitation
from the University of Heidelberg. His brother George,
the mayor of Bretten, had also gone there to meet him.
Here Melanchthon received the news of his wife's death.
Camerarius brought this news to him, and he records that
Melanchthon only said gently, his eyes upturned to heaven:
" Farewell, soon I shall follow you! " The state of affairs
did not permit him immediately to hurry to Wittenberg;
he had to return to Worms. The representatives of the
South German churches expected that he would compose a
unifying confession for them, but Melanchthon declined.
The last hope was a general synod, but it still seemed too
early to discuss such an action. Too many misunderstandings yet remained. With the declarations that he had made
in Worms, Melanchthon himself had again placed the Lu-
therans' friendly relation to the Swiss in question. Here,
too, he was not interested in a literary war.

The religious colloquy at Worms had paraded the split
in the Evangelical side before the eyes of all. In these circumstances even the Evangelical estates were not interested
in a synod. That Melanchthon had to make the proposals
for it was certain. His suggestion was that first the princes
should come to an understanding of what position they intended to maintain. Upon the election of Ferdinand as emperor the princes subscribed the *Frankfurt Recess,* in
which they united in Melanchthonian views on the questions regarding Osiander, good works, the Lord's Supper,
and adiaphora. That the Flacians would take an opposing
position was foreseen. Melanchthon was of the opinion that
a union with them was no longer possible. When the *Weimar Confutation* was published from their side, Melanchthon wrote a clear memorandum, but thought it better not
to print it, in order not to extend the quarrel.

It is true that the irenical and moderate manner of Melanchthon no longer corresponded to the spirit of the time. Quarreling and mutual anathematizing had gained such headway that they could not be stopped. As often as Melanchthon was summoned as a mediator and reconciler, he did not succeed now in bringing peace. One example for many was the Heidelberg Eucharistic controversy in 1559, when Melanchthon had to deliver his opinion, in which he took thoroughly into account the conditions in his Palatine homeland. This memorandum gave the Flacians occasion to attack Melanchthon even beyond the grave.

If Melanchthon had to endure a great deal of hostility within his own ranks during his last years, this did not diminish the frequency with which he was asked for counsel and clarification both from lands beyond Germany and from within the empire. His name carried weight, and he was regarded by many as an authority. To be sure, Melanchthon had never claimed to be such an authority; he was well aware how much he, too, could err. And yet, he was even now the only man in a position to draw up declarations, opinions, and confessions with skill and force. Frequently the question pressed upon him: Who in Evangelical Christendom could issue an authoritative decision? During Luther's lifetime the theological faculty in Wittenberg had this high esteem, and everyone bowed to its judgment. But the situation had changed considerably since Luther's death. Melanchthon's position was thereby made more difficult. There no longer remained a judicature that could speak with full authority. Decisions had to be made, however, especially as the quarrels and controversies multiplied. Some of the Evangelical princes held that theological disputes should be settled by synods. This, indeed, was sometimes done. In his last years Melanchthon no longer agreed with this plan. He thought that synods might multiply the difficulties still more. He now advocated, instead, replacing the synod with an official body of doctrine *(corpus doctrinae)*. Melanchthon indeed had a high regard for the territorial synod, but he did not wish to place a synod at the summit of the whole church. In this judgment the princes did not agree with him. They preferred a general synod.

When a general synod at Frankfurt was proposed, Melanchthon called upon the princes to hold small conferences instead. Great synods, he thought, should take place only very seldom. These ought to be carefully prepared for, in order to prevent splits. The more deeply he penetrated into the scenes of the church's past, however, the more he abandoned all hope of fruitful work on the part of a synod. Ultimately he preferred a standing authority, along the lines of a consistory.

18. His Final Testimony and His Last Days

In the last years of his life Melanchthon still had frequent occasion to occupy himself with the teaching of the Roman Church. Besides the debate which he waged both in writing and orally with the two turncoats, Theobald Thamer, once professor in Marburg, and his own pupil Frederick Staphylus, professor in Königsberg, the Preceptor also had to sharpen his polemical pen against the Jesuits who were active in Bavaria. The occasion was a questionnaire with 31 questions which the latter sent to the Evangelicals in order to induce them to forsake their faith. Melanchthon was so irritated by the method and the procedure of the Jesuits that he took it upon himself to publish the questionnaire, fitted out with a pithy introduction.

He also realized, however, that in addition a detailed refutation of the adversaries was needed. He wrote a whole book, which he dedicated to the Count Palatine Wolfgang, in which he attacked not only Roman dogma, but also Flacians, Anabaptists, and Anti-Trinitarians into the bargain. The *Reply to the Bavarian Inquisition* appeared in August, 1559.

In this controversy Melanchthon proceeds from the concept of the church. He relates himself to the Augsburg Confession and *Apology*, but he draws out his thoughts still further. He who rightly uses Word and Sacrament belongs to the church. As in the parables of the tares and of the net (Matt., ch. 13), both good and bad are found there. In their midst, however, Christ himself is at work through the office that preaches reconciliation. Such outward marks as succession and external authority are not of primary importance, but Word, Sacrament, and — Melanchthon here names as a third mark — obedience to the churchly office. He also examines the objections of the adversaries that the Evangelicals recognize no visible church but appeal only to the church of faith. The church, however, is no Platonic idea; it also has a bodily form. Its unity is assured by the fact that it holds to Christ, not to ecclesiastical customs and uses. While thus demarcating his position from Roman Catholicism, to which he does not ascribe the character of the true church, Melanchthon also uses this opportunity to clear up misunderstandings which had arisen within the Evangelical camp. When he goes into the question of free will, he emphasizes that his conception is a basically different one from that represented in the Catholic Church. He sets forth the Biblical expressions concerning the activity of man, and from this standpoint establishes his position. The controversy with Roman Catholicism, moreover, is one that concerns the doctrine of justification. In particular he takes pains to show that the Council of Trent with its decree ignored the Biblical truth when it rejected the certainty of faith.

Important for him is the proof that the church fathers have taught otherwise. The proof from tradition attains for him a corresponding importance. The fact that he finds in the fathers of the ancient church the expression " faith alone " (sola fides) strengthens him powerfully in his view. That in his doctrine of good works he is not thinking of merit in the Catholic sense should be self-evident. In this realm he is rather settling accounts with the Antinomians.

The *Reply to the Bavarian Inquisition* was the last confession of Melanchthon. It contained his renunciation also of the Catholic conceptions of the Mass, the invocation of saints, and purgatory. At the end of his life he explained with all possible sharpness that these doctrines were not tolerable from the standpoint of the gospel. This writing was intended to be more than an example of current pamphleteering. Even on his deathbed Melanchthon said that it was his final testimony. The *Reply to the Bavarian Inquisition* was received with enthusiasm and found a wide circulation.

In the same way Melanchthon wished to compose one more summary of Evangelical doctrine before his departure. This was apparent in his final revision of the *Loci theologici.* However, since the Leipzig Consistory desired a collection of his writings, he gathered his most important works into a *Corpus doctrinae.* It is revealing to observe what writings he regarded as the most important and selected for this collection: the altered Augsburg Confession, the *Apology,* the Saxon Confession, the *Loci* in their latest edition, the *Examination of Ordinands,* the *Reply to the*

Bavarian Inquisition and finally the *Declaration Regarding the Doctrines of Stancar.* In the preface he wrote: " As God has given me grace, I have earnestly sought to present in a clear and orderly fashion the sum of Christian doctrine, and I have passed over unnecessary, complicated disputes, for disputing also must have a limit."

This preface he wrote on his sixty-third birthday. Imperturbably he remained active, writing letters, delivering lectures, and engaging in conversations. Thoughts of death occupied him. On a little sheet of paper he wrote why he did not fear death. On the left side stood the words:

> You will be redeemed from sin,
> And set free from cares and from the fury
>   of theologians.

On the right side:

> You come to the light, you will look upon God
>   and his Son,
> You will understand the wonderful mysteries
> Which you could not comprehend in this life:
> Why we were so made, and not otherwise,
> And in what the union of the two natures
>   in Christ consists.

Melanchthon had consumed himself in labor to the very end of his days. Early in April, 1560, he traveled once more to Leipzig to examine the recipients of stipends. On the return journey he contracted a grave illness. He developed a high fever. Soon he was terribly weakened. In spite of everything, however, he went to the university until Easter and delivered his lectures. He also labored as usual at home and fulfilled his ordinary duties, attending the academic senate, writing letters, and so on. On Maundy Thursday he attended Holy Communion. On Good Friday he held devotions for foreign students on Isa., ch. 53.

On the next day his friend Camerarius, who had been summoned from Leipzig, found him already exhausted. The devotions that he wished to hold on Easter morning for the foreign students were beyond his strength. True, the fever abated at times, so that he could again write a letter. On April 14 came a messenger from Pomerania, bringing him letters and Jacob Runge's funeral oration for the deceased Duke Philip. This news moved the Master deeply. He remembered the Pomeranian dukes, and what he had once experienced with them, in Heidelberg in 1511 or in Torgau in 1536. In those days they had been the brilliant center of wedding celebrations; now Duke Philip was dead — and he, the other Philip, must follow him. This he surmised, this he knew. The constellation of the stars told him, as well as this beckoning from Pomerania. Melanchthon wrote three more letters to Pomerania and a letter to Duke Albert of Prussia, laying upon his heart the future of the Evangelical Church. Why Duke Albert in particular? Not only because he had occasion to write him at just this time. He knew this prince, and regarded him as a convinced Christian, as a ruler who, to be sure, stood outside the empire and was declared under the ban by the empire, who, however, did all the more for the church and for the people. Moreover, had not Albert shown, despite his partiality toward his spiritual father Andrew Osiander, that he wished to remain faithful to the true gospel, constant and loyal?

Since Melanchthon seemed to be better again on April 16, Camerarius made his departure. With great fervor Melanchthon kept thinking of this most loyal friend of his. With him he had had good conversations, and Camerarius' presence had been able to calm his spirit. Suddenly on the following day the fever returned, so that he began to bid farewell to his friends, and he wished once more to dictate his last will, but he was unable to do so.

The burden of his last prayers was for the unity of the church. For this unity he had worked. With this thought of unity he also wished to die. The words of John 17:11, " that they may be one," were never out of his mind. He also received news of the persecutions in France, which disturbed him greatly. He prayed God to preserve the church, the school, and the government in these lands, which had been purified by his spirit and confirmed in true knowledge. When his favorite passages of Scripture were recited to him, he answered in the same way. To the question whether he desired anything else, he replied, " Nothing but heaven." While his friends prayed and while hundreds of students stood outside the house, he expired about seven o'clock on the evening of April 19, 1560. Peacefully departed the life of the man whom contemporaries in gratitude called " the Preceptor of Germany."

Postscript

A Word About Melanchthon Research

Philip Melanchthon's contemporaries spoke of him as the " teacher of Germany " (*Praeceptor Germaniae*). This title in itself reveals the great importance that was ascribed to him in the life of the German people. With this honor, which no other man received before or after him, Melanchthon occupies a uniquely exalted position. He was incontestably one of the leaders of his century in the world of scholarship, a man of comprehensive and universal mind, who was equally at home in classical philology and philosophy and in theology. Beyond these, he interested himself in all branches of knowledge, whether mathematics or medicine. He was the determining educational influence in Protestant Germany. Church and school considered it an honor to claim him as their own. As author of the standard Evangelical confession, the Augsburg Confession and its *Apology,* as well as the leading textbook of theology, *Loci praecipui theologici,* he took a prominent place in the Evangelical Church of the Reformation era, and was recognized as a standard authority. Though he always stood in the last place even within the Wittenberg faculty because out of modesty he declined the rank of doctor of theology, nevertheless, it was generally known that the initiative frequently proceeded from him, that he possessed the fluent pen and the happy knack of appropriate expression, so that

151

the most important decisions and opinions as a rule came
from him. Even Luther's death did not alter this situation.
Melanchthon was still the leader, even when some of his
former students attacked him, and when through the inept-
ness of others of his students he was drawn into controversies and quarrels. Melanchthon remained the Preceptor
for all.

Not only is this judgment corroborated by his many
memoranda and letters; it also comes to expression in the
addresses on the occasion of his death, and finally in the
comprehensive Latin biography, *A Narration of the Life of
Philip Melanchthon,* written by his intimate friend Joachim Camerarius, 1566 (new edition with numerous an-
notations by G. Th. Strobel, Halle, 1777). This account of
his life strongly shaped the admiring judgment of posterity
and spread his fame no less than his textbooks and addresses.

While the seventeenth century prized his philosophical
works and reissued them repeatedly (cf. P. Petersen's book
on the history of Aristotelian philosophy in Protestant Germany, Jena, 1921), and while, on the other hand, men pursued their theological labors ever more comprehensively
upon the foundation of his *Loci,* the eighteenth century
again yielded him its appreciation as an educator and humanist. Then the historical approach to his views became
popular, and a historical presentation was made of his individual works, especially of the *Loci,* e.g., by Balthasar.

At the middle of the eighteenth century arose the most
important Melanchthon scholar, without whose preliminary work the great *Corpus Reformatorum* edition of
Bretschneider could not have been begun. This unique
man, G. Th. Strobel, in Altdorf, not only assembled the
greatest Melanchthon library at Nuremberg, the city where

the Melanchthonian spirit was fostered, but also succeeded in clarifying his image at many points through a profusion of individual studies. That he was able to awaken an interest in Melanchthon was due to his establishment of a special series, Neue Beiträge zur Literatur des 16. Jahrhunderts, which was filled exclusively with his investigations on Melanchthon.

The rising neohumanism reached back to this preliminary work. Now the time seemed ripe for a closer investigation of Melanchthon. There appeared even a German translation of Melanchthon's most important writings, selected for general use, edited by F. A. Köthe in 1829. In this period, research devoted itself both to the philosopher and now particularly to Melanchthon the theologian, whereby his person and his doctrine aroused special interest. Karl Matthes wrote a biography in 1841, while Neander, Schwarz, Galle, Gass, and Heppe tried to evaluate him from the dogmatic standpoint. The anniversary year, 1860, gave a renewed impulse to this interest. Among the host of occasional writings, including those by Dorner, Kahnis, Planck, and Richard Rothe, the most solid is the one by W. Beyschlag; it was reissued in 1897 in a second edition, and in 1917 in a fourth. On this occasion appeared also the biographies by Moritz Meurer and Carl Schmidt. The latter (Elberfeld, 1861) is to be regarded even to the present day as the most thorough portrayal of Melanchthon's life, although in it the humanist is unquestionably underestimated. The year 1870 brought the first summary work in the *Jahrbücher für deutsche Theologie, Studien zur Theologie Melanchthons,* by A. Herrlinger (published in book form, 1879), but at the same time the frost fell on the first blooms.

It was Albrecht Ritschl's negative judgment that dealt

a heavy blow to Melanchthon research, from which it took many decades to recover. While the Ritschlian school shunned Melanchthon and saw in him simply the corrupter of Luther's theology, only a few men continued their work without troubling themselves over this categorical judgment. From the standpoint of the history of ideas, W. Dilthey undertook to define precisely the position of Melanchthon. In particular the educator Karl Hartfelder distinguished himself by investigating Melanchthon the humanist, and wrote a significant work on Melanchthon as the Preceptor of Germany (1889), adding a bibliography. For the first time since the efforts of M. Mylius, *Chronologia scriptorum Phil. Melanchthonis* (Görlitz, 1582), and Strobel (1777), a comprehensive modern bibliography was attempted. As we know today, this effort also is very incomplete, but still of incomparable value for scholars.

The Melanchthon Jubilee of 1897 again produced some notable addresses, among which should be mentioned those of R. Seeberg and P. Tschackert. The best and most thorough studies of Ferdinand Cohrs and Karl Sell appeared in the *Schriften des Vereins für Reformationsgeschichte*. No German university at that time neglected to hold a Melanchthon celebration, and in this way to underscore the importance of the Reformer. This jubilee year had a special result, insofar as the aforementioned society (*Verein*) resolved to begin the enlargement and completion of the *Corpus Reformatorum* and to establish the *Supplementa Melanchthoniana*. Johannes Haussleiter published Melanchthon's Disputation Theses and other material, and several previously unknown letters also came to light in this period. Forty years after the bulky biography of Carl Schmidt there now appeared in 1902 a belated fruit of the commemorative festival, a biographical sketch of

Philip Melanchthon by Georg Ellinger. From the school of
R. Seeberg followed some dissertations of uneven value,
until Otto Ritschl in his *Dogmengeschichte des Protestan-
tismus,* Vols. I and II (1908–1912), began to concentrate
solidly upon Melanchthon's theological teachings, while
R. Seeberg devoted himself to this theme in his *Dogmengeschichte,* Vol. IV–2 (1920).

The 1930 Jubilee of the Augsburg Confession revived
interest in Melanchthon studies. Not only were the historical contexts discussed anew, but questions in the realms
of political science and social ethics were also taken up.
The best experts on Melanchthon — Werner Elert and
Hans Emil Weber — made weighty contributions to Melanchthon research in their ambitiously conceived works.
Elert in his *Morphologie des Luthertums* (1931, tr. *The
Structure of Lutheranism*) placed Melanchthon in proximity to Luther and emphasized his importance for the
total development of Lutheran theology. His view of
Melanchthon had a stimulating and beneficial influence.
Weber's work, *Reformation, Orthodoxie und Rationalis-
mus* (1937–1952), has proved less popular, but requires
further attention.

Hans Engelland attempted to embrace the entire world
of the Reformer's theological thought in a voluminous
work, *Melanchthon, Glauben und Handeln* (1931),
Broadly conceived, it was an impressive achievement. Engelland's work, however, had little effect; at many points
imposing a preconceived pattern, it unduly flattened out
many features in Melanchthon's views.

The most recent research has related itself to works of
the 1930's. Georg Hoffmann had presented substantial ob-
servations on the Augsburg Confession and the connection between Luther and Melanchthon. Wilhelm Maurer

has taken up this line again, treating individual questions
of Melanchthonian theology in a series of essays. On the
four hundred fiftieth anniversary of the Reformer's birth
Heinrich Bornkamm published a sketch of Melanchthon's
life (1947, 2d ed.); to the influence of Bornkamm and
F. K. Schumann is to be traced the Study Edition of Melanchthon's works, whose editor, the author of this book,
has devoted himself to Melanchthon's understanding of
the church and his views of church polity. In the appendix
of his book, *Der unbekannte Melanchthon,* are reprinted
several writings of Melanchthon's which are lacking in the
Corpus Reformatorum. The author's numerous investigations into various problems of Melanchthon research are to
be gathered into a single volume.

Some other gratifying works have been issued in the past
few years. Wilhelm Neuser has taken up some suggestions
of Th. Hoppe and treated the beginnings of Melanchthon's
theological thought (1950). Paul Schwarzenau attacked the
difficult question of the shift in his theological outlook
(1956). Following the impulse of H. Bornkamm, H. J. Sick
investigated Melanchthon's Old Testament hermeneutic.
Finally, Adolf Sperl has presented a solid work on Melanchthon's position between humanism and Reformation.

Among scholars in other lands at work in this field must
be mentioned Clyde Manschreck in the United States and
Peter Fraenkel in Geneva, Switzerland.

Since Melanchthon was the basic theologian in Wittenberg, the first collection of his works in four volumes was
published as early as 1541 in Basel. Through the influence
of his son-in-law Peucer an enlarged collection followed in
the 1550's. A complete edition, however, has not been produced to this day. C. G. Bretschneider, who began the publication of the *Corpus Reformatorum* in 1834, had intended to edit Melanchthon's *opera omnia.* But as a result

of his death and the inadequate continuation of the edition by Bindseil, this plan remained unfulfilled. The 28-volume Melanchthon edition is only a torso. Many of his works are completely omitted, others are printed only in an edition by later hands, while the important first editions themselves have been left out of account. The editing, moreover, was in many respects inadequately carried through. Necessary references and verifications are lacking. It is surely time to produce a new Melanchthon *corpus,* since the defective edition of *Corpus Reformatorum* must be regarded merely as an emergency aid. In 1874, H. E. Bindseil had edited a supplementary volume with letters and memoranda. It contained, however, only a fraction of the material. Only after the Melanchthon Jubilee of 1897 did the *Verein für Reformationsgeschichte,* under the presidency of Kawerau, Loofs, and later Hans von Schubert, resolve to produce the *Supplementa Melanchthoniana,* which were to fill in the *Corpus Reformatorum* on all sides. In this collection, four volumes appeared between 1910 and 1926. However, when Otto Clemen resigned the editorship of the *Supplementum* in order to work on Luther's correspondence, this valuable project fell into abeyance. It is scarcely thinkable that after a generation it could be revived. What we need today is no emergency aid, but a great, complete Melanchthon edition.

Presently available is only a Study Edition in six volumes, which contains the most important writings of Melanchthon in their original versions. Like the well-known Clemen Edition of Luther's works, it is designed primarily for student use, and is therefore characterized as a Study Edition. In many instances it goes beyond the *Corpus Reformatorum* and even offers writings which the *Corpus Reformatorum* lacks. It presents a better text edited according to the first printings, and in the case of often reprinted works it also identifies variant readings.

Now in preparation are also the German versions of his principal works. The translation of the *Loci communes* prepared by George Spalatin in 1522 is in print; to follow this volume is the German version of his *Loci praecipui theologici* on which Melanchthon himself worked in 1552. This edition will be produced on the basis of his autographs rediscovered in Olmütz, Moravia. Next, a new Melanchthon bibliography is to be prepared. Without a new working tool of this kind it is impossible to verify the extent of Melanchthon's literary productivity. If the most important printings of the Reformer's works are contained in the two great Melanchthon libraries, viz., that of the Melanchthon House in Bretten, founded by Nikolaus Müller in 1903, and the city library in Nuremberg, which houses the Melanchthon collection of G. Th. Strobel, it must nevertheless be kept in mind that many of these editions, and particularly the autographs of Melanchthon, are scattered all over the world. Besides the Vatican Library in Rome are to be mentioned especially the many great libraries in the United States. A systematic inventory of all autographs and printed editions has never been attempted. It must be undertaken, however, in order to prepare the way for the coming great Melanchthon edition.

The most urgent task of Melanchthon research is presently the reediting of his correspondence. In the Center for Melanchthon Research in Heidelberg the foundation has been laid for this work. It would require the lifetime of a single scholar. This task is therefore to be entrusted to a group of scholars. The corpus of correspondence will far exceed in amount the eleven-volume Luther correspondence. The number of more than seven thousand letters and memoranda which were published in *Corpus Refor-*

matorum, Vols. I to X (1834–1842) will be increased probably by 50 percent through the addition of the epistolary material published within the last 125 years.

In an age that loved correspondence Melanchthon was one of the most zealous letter writers. It is well known how skillful he was in using the couriers who stood at his command, whether traveling scholars, students, or professional letter carriers. When he had a messenger available, he immediately wrote up to ten letters. For this reason the news that he passed on to his friends was frequently the same. In many letters the section concerned with current events is identical. Since a part of Melanchthon's letters was " adapted " before publication even in the sixteenth century, i.e., abbreviated or even altered in wording, the copies must be painstakingly reexamined and traced through their transmission. Many letters are current in several copies, whose variants must be established. The information given by Bretschneider unfortunately is not always reliable.

Experience teaches that many libraries and archives still contain unpublished letters of Melanchthon. Individual unprinted letters are still found in private possession. For this reason a systematic general inquiry within and outside of Germany is necessary. A new bibliography will make it possible for the first time to obtain a survey of the entire correspondence, which has been so disintegrated and scattered, often published in scarcely accessible journals. This edition of correspondence is so pressing a requirement for further research that international Reformation research can scarcely neglect it any longer. This will yield the foundation for the equally urgent great biography of Melanchthon.

Selected Bibliography in English

MELANCHTHON'S WORKS

The Loci Communes of Philip Melanchthon, tr. by Charles L. Hill (the 1521 edition). Meador Publishing Company, 1944. A new translation by Lowell J. Satre is to appear in The Library of Christian Classics, Vol. XIX, *Melanchthon and Bucer,* ed. by Wilhelm Pauck, to be published by The Westminster Press and the SCM Press, Ltd., London.

Melanchthon: On Christian Doctrine, ed. and tr. by Clyde L. Manschreck. Oxford University Press, 1965. This is the 1555 edition of the *Loci.*

Melanchthon: Selected Writings, tr. by Charles L. Hill; ed. by E. E. Flack and L. J. Satre. Augsburg Publishing House, 1962. Contains eleven short writings.

The Augsburg Confession (1530), *The Apology of the Augsburg Confession* (1531), and the *Treatise on the Power and Primacy of the Pope* (1537) appear in *The Book of Concord,* ed. by Theodore G. Tappert. Muhlenberg Press, 1959.

The Variata (Altered) Editions of the Augsburg Confession (1540 and 1542), *Opinion of Philip Melanchthon Concerning the Foundation of the Doctrine of the Sacramentarians* (1530), *The Wittenberg Concord* (1536), and *Leipsic Interim* (1548), in Vol. 2 of *The Book of Concord,* ed. by Henry E. Jacobs. 2 volumes. G. W. Frederick, 1882–1883.

Instruction to the Visitors (1528), in Vol. 40 of *Luther's Works,* American Edition, ed. by Jaroslav Pelikan and Helmut T. Lehmann. Concordia Publishing House and Muhlenberg Press, 1958.

The Wittenberg Articles (1536), in *The Lutheran movement in England,* by Henry E. Jacobs. G. W. Frederick, 1894, pp. 66–67.

The Augsburg Confession, ed. and tr. by J. M. Reu. Wartburg Publishing House, 1930. Among the excellent collection of documents are several items by Melanchthon.

"The Debate Between Eck and Melanchthon," tr. by Heinz Mackensen in *Lutheran Quarterly,* 1959. Abridged version of the Colloquy of Worms, 1540.

Reply to Pico della Mirandola (1558), tr. by Quirinus Breen in *Journal of the History of Ideas,* 1552.

Preface to the Basel Edition of *Euclid's Geometry* (1537), tr. by M. A. Moore, in *Isis,* 1959.

On Orion (1553), tr. by William Hammer, in "Melanchthon, Inspirer of the Study of Astronomy," *Popular Astronomy,* 1951.

Excerpts from Melanchthon's Works

Bainton, Roland H., *The Age of the Reformation.* D. Van Nostrand Company, Inc., 1956. (Anvil Book.)

Fosdick, Harry Emerson (ed.), *Great Voices of the Reformation.* Modern Library, Inc., 1952.

Kidd, Beresford James, *Documents Illustrative of the Continental Reformation.* Oxford University Press, 1911.

Manschreck, Clyde L., *A History of Christianity* (Vol. 2, *Readings in the History of the Church from the Reformation to the Present*). Prentice-Hall, Inc., 1964.

——— *Prayers of the Reformers.* Muhlenberg Press, 1958. Contains several prayers of Melanchthon.

Biography

Hill, Charles L. (ed.), *The Loci Communes.* Meador Publishing Company, 1944. Introduction gives a chapter on Melanchthon's life.

Manschreck, Clyde L., *Melanchthon, the Quiet Reformer.* Abingdon Press, 1958. The only recent full-length biography in English. Extremely sympathetic.

Richard, James W., *Philip Melanchthon, the Protestant Pre-*

ceptor of Germany. G. P. Putnam's Sons, 1898. A solid piece of work in its day.

Articles on Melanchthon in:

The New Schaff-Herzog Encyclopedia of Religious Knowledge

Encyclopædia Britannica

Lutheran Cyclopedia

The Encyclopedia of the Lutheran Church

ESSAYS FROM THE 400TH ANNIVERSARY OF MELANCHTHON'S DEATH, 1960

Vajta, Vilmos (ed.), *Luther and Melanchthon.* Muhlenberg Press, 1961. Papers of the Second International Congress on Luther Research, Münster, Westphalia, 1960. Essays in English:

Pauck, Wilhelm, " Luther and Melanchthon." Best treatment of this theme in English.

Grimm, Harold J., " The Relations of Luther and Melanchthon with the Townsmen." Documents the spread of the Reformation in the free towns.

Fraenkel, Peter, " Ten Questions Concerning Melanchthon, the Fathers and the Eucharist." A penetrating study in Melanchthon's methodology and theology.

Tappert, Theodore G., " Melanchthon in America." The image of Melanchthon in American Lutheran history.

Another article in this volume has been translated by Robert C. Schultz in *Dialog* (Minneapolis), 1963: " A Comparison of Melanchthon's and Luther's Doctrine of Justification, Haikola, Lauri."

In *Lutheran World* (Geneva), September, 1960:

Maurer, Wilhelm, " Melanchthon as Author of the Augsburg Confession."

Stupperich, Robert, " The Development of Melanchthon's Theological-Philosophical World View." Essays by Germany's two leading Melanchthon scholars.

In *Concordia Theological Monthly* (St. Louis), August and September, 1960:

Lueker, Erwin L., " Luther and Melanchthon."

Meyer, Carl S., " Melanchthon as Educator and Humanist."

Piepkorn, Arthur C., " Melanchthon the Confessor."

Preus, Robert D., " Melanchthon the Theologian."

Thiele, Gilbert A., " Melanchthon the Churchman."

In *Archiv für Reformationsgeschichte* (Gütersloh), 1960. In English:

Manschreck, Clyde L., " Melanchthon and Prayer."

GENERAL INTERPRETATIONS AND BROADER TOPICS

(See also " Essays from the 400th Anniversary of Melanchthon's Death, 1960," above.)

Caemmerer, Richard C., " The Melanchthonian Blight," in *Concordia Theological Monthly*, 1947, Vol. 5. Sharply hostile.

Elert, Werner, *The Structure of Lutheranism*, tr. by Walter A. Hansen. Concordia Publishing House, 1962. An older classic (1931), which attempts to place Luther and Melanchthon in the context of developing Lutheranism.

Green, Lowell C., " Luther and Melanchthon," in *The Mature Luther*, ed. by Theodore G. Tappert. Augsburg Publishing House, 1959.

Hildebrandt, Franz, *Melanchthon: Alien or Ally?* The Macmillan Company, 1946. Analyzes the question, but does not finally answer it.

Hill, Charles L., ed., *The Loci Communes.* Meader Publishing Company, 1944. Introduction presents an aggressively sympathetic interpretation.

Lentz, Harold H., *Reformation Crossroads.* Augsburg Publishing House, 1958. An effort, based on modern authors, to indicate the significance of Luther and Melanchthon for present-day theology.

Pauck, Wilhelm, " Luther and Melanchthon." (See above, under " Essays from the 400th Anniversary of Melanchthon's Death, 1960.")

Pelikan, Jaroslav, *From Luther to Kierkegaard.* Concordia Publishing House, 1950. Interpretation of the history of philosophical thinking within Lutheranism.

Schultz, Robert C., " Melanchthon After Four Hundred Years," in *Cresset* (Valparaiso, Indiana) , 1960. Brief popular article.

Schwiebert, Ernest G., " New Groups and Ideas at the University of Wittenberg," in *Archiv für Reformationsgeschichte,* 1958. Indicates Melanchthon's place in the "first Protestant university."

SPECIAL STUDIES IN THEOLOGY

(See also works dealing with the Lutheran Confessions, e.g., in *Concordia Theological Monthly.*)

Bakhuizen van den Brink, J. N., " Bible and Biblical Theology in the Early Reformation," in *Scottish Journal of Theology,* 1961–1962.

Bente, F., and Dau, W. (eds.) , *Concordia Triglotta.* Concordia Publishing House, 1921. Still valuable for detailed discussion of theological controversies within Lutheranism. Conservative Lutheran viewpoint.

Clark, Francis, S.J., *Eucharistic Sacrifice and the Reformation.* The Newman Press, 1960. Roman Catholic critique of Protestant interpretations.

Fraenkel, Peter, *Revelation and Tradition.* Lund, 1959. (*Studia Theologica.*) Subtitle: Notes on Some Aspects of Doctrinal Continuity in the Theology of Philip Melanchthon.

———, *Testimonia Patrum.* Gregory Lounz, 1961. (*Travaux d'Humanisme et Renaissance.*) Subtitle: The Function of the Patristic Argument in the Theology of Philip Melanchthon.

McNeill, John T., " Natural Law in the Teaching of the Reformers," in *Journal of Religion,* 1946. Devotes a section to Melanchthon.

Manschreck, Clyde L., " The Bible in Melanchthon's Philosophy of Education," in *Journal of Bible and Religion,* 1955.

———, " The Role of Melanchthon in the Adiaphora Controversy," in *Archiv für Reformationsgeschichte,* 1957. Condensation of a Yale dissertation, which is available on microcard.

———, " Reason and Conversion in the Thought of Melanchthon," in Franklin H. Littell (ed.), *Reformation Studies* (Bainton Festschrift). John Knox Press, 1962.

Oyer, John, " The Writings of Melanchthon Against the Anabaptists," in *Mennonite Quarterly Review,* 1952. Condensation of a Chicago dissertation, available on microfilm.

———, *Lutheran Reformers Against Anabaptists: Luther, Melanchthon and Menius and the Anabaptists of Central Germany.*

Wiswedel, W., and Friedmann, R., " The Anabaptists Answer Melanchthon," in *Mennonite Quarterly Review,* 1955. English translation and analysis of an Anabaptist " Handbook " of 1558.

SPECIAL STUDIES ON PHILOSOPHY, SCIENCE, METHOD, AND TEXTS

Breen, Quirinus, " The Twofold Truth Theory in Melanchthon," in *Review of Religion,* 1945, Vol. 1. By an expert in the field of humanism.

———, " The Terms ' Loci Communes ' and ' Loci ' in Melanchthon," in *Church History,* 1947.

———, " The Subordination of Philosophy to Rhetoric in Melanchthon," in *Archiv für Reformationsgeschichte,* 1952. Analyzes the Reply to Pico.

———, " Some Aspects of Humanistic Rhetoric and the Reformation," in *Nederlands Archief voor Kerkgeschiedenis,* 1959. Brings together the author's findings from several other essays.

———, " Melanchthon's Sources for a Life of Agricola," in *Archiv für Reformationsgeschichte,* 1961. Viz. Rudolf Agricola, the early German humanist.

Gilbert, Neal W., *Renaissance Concepts of Method.* Columbia University Press, 1960. Contains an analysis of Melanchthon's views.

Hammer, William, " Melanchthon, Inspirer of Astronomy," in *Popular Astronomy,* 1951.

Ong, Walter J., S.J., *Ramus. Method and the Decay of Dialogue.* Harvard University Press, 1958. Analyzes Melanchthon's views on method.

Salomon, R., " The Teuffenbach Copy of Melanchthon's Loci
    Communes," in *Renaissance News,* 1955. Manuscript anal-
    ysis.
Stupperich, Robert, " What Does Melanchthon's Genuine Au-
    tograph Concerning John 14:23 Look Like? " in *Mediae-
    valia et Humanistica,* 1963.

Index of Names and Subjects

Index of Melanchthon's Writings

(The identification of writings is not exhaustive. English translations are listed where available. Otherwise the originals are cited, usually in the latest edition.)

ABBREVIATIONS:

BC — *Book of Concord,* ed. by T. E. Tappert (Philadelphia, 1959) ; ed. by H. E. Jacobs, 2 vols. (Philadelphia, 1882 f.)

CR — *Corpus Reformatorum, Ph. Melanthonis Opera,* ed. by Bretschneider and Bindseil, 28 vols. (Halle, 1834 ff.)

LCC — *Library of Christian Classics,* Vol. XIX: *Melanchthon and Bucer* (Vol. in preparation, The Westminster Press)

LW — *Luther's Works* ("American Edition"), ed. by J. Pelikan and H. T. Lehmann (St. Louis and Philadelphia, 1955 ff.)

MW — *Melanchthons Werke in Auswahl* ("Student Edition"), ed. by R. Stupperich, 6 vols. (Gütersloh, 1951 ff.)

SM — *Supplementa Melanchthoniana,* ed. by O. Clemen, 6 vols. (Leipzig, 1910 ff.)

UM — *Der Unbekannte Melanchthon,* by R. Stupperich (Stuttgart, 1961)

WA — *Luthers Werke* ("Weimarer Ausgabe"), (Weimar, 1883 ff.)